Waltham Forest Public Libraries

PS168

Please return this item by
the last date stamped.
The loan may be renewed
unless required by
another reader.

Walthamstow Library
High Street
Walthamstow
London E17 7JN
Tel: **0208 4961100**

MAR 07

4 MAY 2007

11 OCT 2007

29 MAY 2007

0 2 JUL 2007

2 0 JUL 2007

1 3 MAY 2010

D1513847

WALTHAM FOREST LIBRARIES

027 328 179

This book is dedicated to my parents
Jan Mohammed Khan (rest in peace)
and Hanifa Begum Khan.

Thanks, mum and dad, for everything you
have given me in life. Thanks for making
Britain our home, giving me the opportunity
of a free education and the chance to be whom
I want to be. I'll never forget the sacrifices you
made for me. I hope I've made you proud.

Waltham Forest Libraries	
027328179	
Askews	07-Dec-2006
650.1 KHA	£9.99

P.U.S.H.
FOR SUCCESS

Saira Khan

STAR OF *THE APPRENTICE*

Vermilion
LONDON

1 3 5 7 9 10 8 6 4 2

Copyright © Saira Khan 2006

Saira Khan has asserted her moral right to be identified as the author of
this work in accordance with the Copyright, Design and Patents Act 1988.

All rights reserved. No part of this publication may be reproduced,
stored in a retrieval system, or transmitted in any form or by any means,
electronic, mechanical, photocopying, recording or otherwise,
without the prior permission of the copyright owner.

First published in the United Kingdom in 2006 by Vermilion,
an imprint of Ebury Publishing
Random House UK Ltd.
Random House
20 Vauxhall Bridge Road
London SW1V 2SA

Random House Australia (Pty) Limited
20 Alfred Street, Milsons Point, Sydney, New South Wales 2061, Australia

Random House New Zealand Limited
18 Poland Road, Glenfield, Auckland 10, New Zealand

Random House (Pty) Limited
Isle of Houghton, Corner Boundary Road & Carse O'Gowrie,
Houghton, 2198, South Africa

Random House UK Limited Reg. No. 954009
www.randomhouse.co.uk
Papers used by Vermilion are natural, recyclable
products made from wood grown in sustainable forests.

A CIP catalogue record is available for this book from the British Library.

ISBN: 0091910447

Designed and set by seagulls

Printed and bound in Great Britain by
Mackays of Chatham plc, Chatham, Kent

CONTENTS

ACKNOWLEDGEMENTS

This book would not have been possible without the following people, and I am eternally grateful for their help, support and encouragement:

Professional

Clare Hulton – my publishing director: Thank you for believing in me and giving me the opportunity to prove myself. I will never forget the chance you gave me. It means so much.

Julia Kellaway – my editor: You are simply a very talented young lady and it was my privilege to have worked with such a passionate, confident and focused individual. You are the best.

Random House PR, sales and marketing: Your support has been outstanding and you've been so kind to me. Thank you.

Elizabeth Ayto – my agent: You are the hardest-working woman I have ever met. You're great. Thank you.

Alan Chapman and Vicky Chislett: Alan – thanks for creating the best business website out there (www.businessballs.com) and for helping me with the learning style questionnaire. Both you and Vicky delivered the product on time. You were a joy to work with.

Family

Steven Hyde: I love you. Thanks for being with me through thick and thin, and for believing in me. You're my rock. You've helped me become a better person and you've shown me the power of love. I could not have done this without your support and love.

Mum: You're my inspiration and motivation; you're my role model. I hope I've made you proud. Love you so much.

Mac and Margaret Hyde: The best mother- and father-in-law anyone could ask for. Your support, guidance and love have been overwhelming. You're so special to me.

Masood, Tariq and Sajdah – my brothers and sister: Your support and love have carried me through the hard times. I love you all very much, and no, you can't have loads of free copies!

Maria, Tim, Lynn, Mark, Sajdah and Rizvi: Thanks for all your support and love. It means so much to me.

Friends

Joanna Steed, Tina Ghaiden, Adrian Newson, Diana Stenning, James Bainbridge, Alison Moss, Henry and Colin, Steph and Lisa, Josephine Fender, Beth Saunt, Jane Hopkins, Simon Natarajan, Amanda and Edward Brown, Ian and Leslie Humphries, Tim Campbell, Adele Locke, Pamela Simms and Stewart Mitchell and Paul Walsh at Bristows. Thanks for being there for me. It's been a roller coaster. I've enjoyed the ride and hope you have too! You've been so very understanding. Thanks.

PREFACE
What Makes Me Tick?

I am a rebel. I like to challenge the status quo and I have no problem with questioning authority. I don't like it when things are unfair. I will go to great lengths to prove that an injustice has occurred and that it needs to be put right.

Was I born a rebel or am I just a product of my environment? Looking back on my life, I think it's a mixture of the two. I know that my early years shaped who and what I am today and what I strive for. Those years were the most painful yet the most memorable. If you want to understand my drive for success, you need to understand the early years of my life.

I always get asked the same questions: 'Where do you get that drive from?' 'Where do you get your confidence from?' 'Where do you get your energy from?' I find it difficult to answer any of these questions without referring to my background and my childhood experiences.

I am the oldest of four children; I have two brothers and one sister. My parents came to England in the 1960s from Kashmir, a war-torn area in the Himalayas between Pakistan and India. They lived in a very poor, rural country but grew up in a culture based on strong family values, where the man was regarded as the leader and provider of the home. They lived in villages with no electricity or mod cons, with the extended family all close by. Water was not piped into homes; my mother recalls a daily chore of women fetching water from local wells, about a mile away, and carrying it back in big pots placed on their heads. Food was locally produced, and most people had chickens, goats and buffalos to tend. It was a very simple but labour-intensive life.

My parents had an arranged marriage, which was customary. My mother had studied up to the equivalent of GCSE level; she wasn't very academic and was 19 when she married. My father, on the other hand, was very bright; he was studying to be a doctor before he decided to go to England and make some money. He was 29 when he married. In 1965, my parents left their whole family – parents, brothers and sisters, uncles and aunts – behind to make a new life for themselves in England. I was born in 1970.

In 1976, my parents bought their first property, a two-up, two-down terraced house. I shared a room with my sister; my brothers shared the other room and my parents slept on a mattress downstairs in the living room. My father worked in a lace factory and my mother did piecework at home. She'd bring home small boxes full of components which she had to assemble. The next day she would take them back and get another box. If she was lucky she'd come back with three boxes; on a bad day it was just the one. When I was eight, I'd help my mum with her piecework whilst the other kids were playing outside. By the age of 11 I was responsible for helping mum clean and tidy the whole house. I became very independent at a young age; by the age of 12 I was responsible for all the housework. My Saturday mornings consisted of making the beds, cleaning the bathroom and kitchen, hoovering and ironing.

Throughout my life I have seen my mother work hard. In 1982 she started working in a factory and every day would go to work, come home, cook a fresh meal, do all the washing up and then prepare her sandwiches for work the next day. My mother used to wake at 5am and walk five miles to work to save her bus fare. She's an incredible woman, and without her example I probably wouldn't have understood the meaning of hard work. She did all she could for us – she attended our school plays, she did the parents' evenings and she'd show off our sports trophies to other parents with pride. She made sure we had a birthday party and didn't miss out on things. Even though we were Muslim, my mum made sure that we celebrated Christmas; she tried her best to help us integrate. Working in a factory with English people helped her to understand English culture.

My father was a very complex man. He had high standards and expectations in life for both himself and his children. My father ruled our house and we were all petrified of him. He only had to look at any of us in a certain way and we'd know we were in trouble. His frustrations with his life and the injustices he had to deal with at work translated into anger and violence, and most of that was taken out on the family. I watched my father lash out at my mother and us children. I remember one time when my parents had decided to visit some friends. They were gone for only about an hour when my mother returned hiding her face. My dad had hit her and she'd got a black eye. He'd got angry at something my mum had said. That's all it took for my dad to lose the plot. I remember feeling so sorry for my mum and very angry at my dad.

I have been hit by a belt, shoes, a cane and a wire coat hanger. I have watched my father break all sorts of household items in anger: the television was flung out of the room once and landed in the garden, smashing into smithereens, because we were watching *Grange Hill* and my father didn't approve. One of my most vivid memories is when my father caught me walking home from school with my socks rolled down at the age of 14. That evening he whipped my legs with a wire coat hanger, yelling that he didn't send me to school to become fashionable but to study. The next day he put me in a school uniform and sent me to school. I was the only girl in my school who wore a uniform; it was a non-uniform school. It took me a very long time to forgive my dad for that. Even now, the painful memory of that event still knots my stomach when I think about it. My father had only one focus for us kids: to study hard, get good grades and go to university. His discipline was so extreme because he wanted us to do well and better ourselves. I was never praised by my dad – growing up all I heard was: 'You're too thin,' 'You're too small,' 'You're too outspoken,' 'You're not as clever as other girls,' 'You're useless in the kitchen,' 'You should cover yourself up more,' 'No, you can't do this' and 'No, you can't do that.'

I wasn't allowed to go out with friends after school; I was never permitted to venture into town by myself; I had no social life after school at all. The only thing my father did allow me to do was play competitive games. I joined all the sports teams as it was a way for me to experience life outside the home. My best friend Joanna Steed (whom I am still very close to) was my link to what English kids were in to: fashion, music, magazines and English life generally. I would call for Joanna every morning to walk with her to school. I loved going into her beautiful home and waiting for her to get ready in her own huge room. She'd let me try on her clothes, and even borrow her trendy Adidas trainers for sports. I'd be wearing my uniform at the age of 16 while Joanna would have the latest clothes and shoes on, with a fashionable hairdo. I used to dream that one day I'd be able to live like that. I hung around girls like Joanna because I wanted what they had.

I was 18 years old when I first ventured on to a train and travelled by myself into town. I had led a very protected and controlled life. I would never say that I had an unhappy childhood – I didn't at all – but I just remember it as quite painful at times. I never felt really relaxed: life was always about working hard and being serious, and there never seemed much time for having a laugh and chilling out.

There was another side to my father: he was one of

the most caring, generous and loving human beings I have ever met. Every day he would spend two hours with us teaching us our mother tongue and making sure we were on top of our homework. He made time for our educational development and was a very hands-on father. If we had 'flu or any kind of illness he would be the one that would make sure that we had the right medicines and look after us, he was the one to drive us around in our six-week holidays and he was the one that ultimately had to deal with everything concerning the family. Having four children and a wife that didn't speak much English, and living on a low wage, and being responsible for all the family decisions could not have been easy for one man to deal with.

My father was open-minded and welcomed people into his home, regardless of their race and religion. His friends in the Asian community would travel from afar to listen to his sense of humour. Deep down, my father was a good man; his biggest fear was that his children would grow up in a Western world and not remember their culture and roots, and he was determined not to let that happen. My father did the best he could under the circumstances; he worked hard and he looked after us. He didn't want us to follow in his footsteps, enduring the same daily hard grind to make ends meet. My father's parents died whilst he was in England and he never made their funeral. I think he always felt very guilty about that, and that's why he became angry. But he was a good man with a good heart. Even though I didn't see him like that at the time, I knew deep down that he meant well for me.

When you grow up in a household where anger is the consistent emotion, you start thinking that it's okay to be angry and to show anger. I don't remember a lot of love being shown in our house: we were a very tightknit family but not in an emotional way. There were no hugs and kisses. I remember being angry at my dad constantly and thinking to myself: 'Why can't he be like other dads and chill out and just be happy? Why is he always so angry?' His behaviour was totally irrational to me.

I became a very angry person. I was angry because my father wouldn't let me be who I wanted to be. I was controlled, and the fact that I was a girl meant that I was controlled even more tightly. I despised this. I hated the fact that as a girl I was told I couldn't wear this or do that, and what was expected of me as an Islamic woman. I led two lives: one was my Western school life and the other was my Asian life at home.

The transformation was a physical one every day. I'd dress for school in a skirt and blouse and come back home and slip into the traditional *salwar kameez* – a long tunic and baggy trousers, designed not to draw attention to a woman's physical shape. I never wore these clothes outside the home; I refused to. At home I ate different food to the meals my English friends ate, and watched Bollywood films whilst my friends were going to the cinema. For holidays, we went to visit relatives in different cities. We never had a holiday abroad; we just couldn't afford it. Even if we could, holidays were not sensible things to waste hard-earned money on. We never ate out as a family – why eat out when it's cheaper to cook food at home? We never spoke English with our parents, only the mother tongue at home.

I grew up in a small town called Long Eaton, which is sandwiched between two cities: Nottingham and Derby. I grew up in a predominantly white area, my friends were white and our neighbours were white. There were a handful of other Asian people in the town but not a significant number. My mum never shopped in local grocery stores because they did not provide her with the ingredients that she was looking for, so every Saturday my parents would drive to Nottingham to shop in the Asian shops for Halal meat and fruits and vegetables to make a curry, such as okra, aubergines and spices. I think growing up in such a white dominant area made me feel so self conscious and at times very uncomfortable, but at the same time it helped me to integrate with people from different backgrounds, religions and cultures. With hindsight, I can see that growing up living two different cultural lives has had its benefits, but as a young kid, feeling so different was very painful and confusing. I was so conscious that my mum looked different to other mums and my dad behaved differently to other dads. I felt I didn't belong to either side.

This sense of injustice made me challenge the Asian way. I challenged my dad and I challenged all the conservative people around him. I was constantly told off by my father for being so outspoken, but I didn't care. To me, it was about standing up for the truth and what I believed in. I remember one Asian woman coming to our house and telling my father that she didn't think me going away to university was a good idea because once I'd been educated I'd be independent and impossible to control. Another time an important member of my mum's family came over from Pakistan to visit. As soon as he arrived he was given the best chair in the house and we had to behave like perfect children; we were warned to speak only when asked a question and not to take the biscuits put out for the guest. He started talking about women, about how they needed to be covered up more, and that here in England he could see some parents were not in control of their kids. I could feel my blood boiling, and even though I knew I'd be in so much trouble I blurted out, 'Well, why should women get covered up? Men should keep their hands to themselves and then women would be all right. Why don't you cover yourself up and see what it feels like?' Across the room I could see my dad give me that look.

Weirdly, my dad did encourage me to debate and stand up for myself. I think he did that because, deep down, he knew I'd have to fight my own corner in life and he was preparing me for that. Luckily for me, my dad was a great advocate of education, and there was no doubt in his mind that I would go to university. My objective was slightly more specific than that: I wanted to go to a university as far away from home as was physically possible.

I went to Brighton Polytechnic when I was 18 but, again, the fact that it was a polytechnic was never good enough for my dad: 'Why can't you go to a university?' However, when the time came for him to drop me off at the halls of residence, he cried, and for the first time in his life gave me a hug. I can still feel that hug; it was so special. You'd think that I would have gone totally wild at university and rebelled against my strict upbringing and the injustice I felt, but I didn't. I didn't touch a drop of alcohol and was never tempted by drugs. The only thing I was focused on was proving to my dad that I was clever and that I could improve myself without going off the rails. I got my degree and then went to Nottingham University to do a Masters, which pleased my dad no end.

I couldn't afford to pay my fees so my dad started to work longer hours in the factory. He was a diabetic and the doctor had told him not to work too hard, but he wanted to, just so I could get my Masters. He had to give up when he collapsed at work one day, and I felt so bad that he was doing it for me.

My favourite memory of my dad is when I'd got my first job as a town planner and drove home in my company car to see my family. He was so happy and I loved him for showing me his happiness. Finally, in my dad's eyes, I had achieved his approval and it meant so much to me. That weekend was so special. I felt I'd finally achieved what he'd wanted and that he was proud. However, I continued to push myself to do better all the time to get his approval. I became addicted to it.

My dad was my focus. I was driven to make him happy and to get his approval. I was doing all I could to demonstrate to him that his decision to leave his family and friends back in Kashmir was not in vain, that he had been successful and could say that his daughter had done well. Just when I was really getting close to my dad and enjoying his company, he died suddenly of a heart attack in 1998.

I was absolutely devastated. I felt that my whole focus and purpose in life was taken away from me in an instant. For the first time I felt really alone, completely responsible for myself and extremely angry with God and the world. The only question I tried to answer in my mind for months was, 'Why did this have to happen to me and my family?'

People say anger is bad, that the emotion needs to be controlled and should never really be shown. Well, I disagree. If it wasn't for my anger I wouldn't have had the will to stand up for myself and push the boundaries. I would never have had the overwhelming urge to prove my worth to those who felt I was a hopeless case. Importantly, I would never have had the drive after my father's death to respect his name and all that he stood for. Anger drives me to do well. My anger has stopped me feeling sorry for myself and my circumstances. I am a strong person because of my anger, instead of being pathetic and blaming the world for my problems and hard upbringing. Anger has made me just get on with it, deal with it and move forward.

As an adult I have less to be angry about. I have controlled my temper and impatience, and the credit has to go to my husband Steve, who hasn't got an angry bone in his body. He has shown me that love can be a more productive and powerful emotion to base my drive on. I wish someone had helped my dad to understand that.

What I find really interesting is that I am not angry with my father. Some people in my position may have focused on all the negatives like the violence and the beatings, but I never held that against my dad. I have always concentrated on the positives. My dad was the way he was because he wanted the best for us; he wanted to show us the right way and he sacrificed his own life to give us that opportunity. I am grateful to him.

I have shared this very personal account with you because I think it will help you to get a better understanding of what makes me tick, and provide a context for the following chapters. More importantly, I hope it will inspire you to understand what makes *you* tick by recalling the events in your life that have shaped who you are today.

Saira Khan

INTRODUCTION

BEING PUSHY IS NOT A SIN

I became known in the media as the 'pushy' one in *The Apprentice*. It became apparent to me that being pushy is not the British way. It's not really seen as a positive attribute and is certainly not to be encouraged.

Well, I want to put a stop to that.

My life experience has taught me a very important lesson: if you don't push you will end up settling for second best and become an average kind of person. I have never been prepared to be second best. Whenever I've felt that I'm being treated as an average person I've just moved on to find a better way. I have taken lots of risks but I believe that by being true to myself and wanting to do better I will achieve the life I want to live and be the person I want to be.

People who watched me on *The Apprentice* have called me a role model. They felt that my energy and positive, proactive and passionate attitude were motivational and inspirational. I have had mothers come up to me in the street and tell me that their young daughters have now decided to go into business because of watching me on the television. Asian women have told me that I have helped to break down the stereotype of Asian women being 'quiet', 'submissive' and 'insignificant'.

The key question I get all the time is: 'Where do you get your energy, confidence and passion from?' My simple answer is from my life experience. There's no special formula. I haven't had any life coaching. I wasn't born with a silver spoon in my mouth and I haven't got any friends in high places. I am like anybody else out there. The difference is that I have pushed myself, believed in myself and never given up on my ability to **gain skills, improve my knowledge** and **adopt a positive attitude.** I have done this by being assertive, knowing what I want and working outside my comfort zone. Above all, I have put effort and hard work into my life. These are the core values my parents gave me, which I have used as my standards in everything I do.

HOW TO BE CONFIDENT

Some people are born confident but many are not. I believe confidence is something that can be learnt and is the key to pushing yourself to do better. People always comment on my confidence; I can get up and give a speech to 300 people without breaking into a sweat, but I couldn't have done so 10 years ago. There are several reasons why I can do it now:

- I have had lots of experience.
- I have been trained to understand how to give presentations.
- I have watched and worked with some great presenters.
- I have asked for feedback to improve myself.
- I have stood in front of a mirror practising and visualising the audience.
- Most of all, I got off my bum and had a go. I made some mistakes at the beginning but I learnt and pushed myself to do better. I never gave up.

You will have noticed that I use the word 'I' a lot. Get used to that – as an adult *I* am the one who has made things happen for *my* self in *my* life. I control my life and all the decisions I make about it, and I take full responsibility for all my actions. I don't like excuses and I don't like to lay the blame elsewhere – it's too easy to do that and a cop-out.

MY P.U.S.H. THEORY

So what does P.U.S.H. stand for and how did I come up with my theory? Well, like all good ideas, it came to me while I was lying in bed one night. I asked my husband Steve how he thought others saw me. His response was:

Well, I think people see you as a pushy, proactive, passionate woman. I think all these qualities make you stand out from a crowd. You are not everyone's cup of tea because these qualities do not sit comfortably with traditional British culture, but you've actually decided you don't care what others think and you have challenged conservative methods and people. If I compare myself to you, I'd say I probably had a lot more going for me, but I just haven't really had to push myself as much as you. I came from a white, middle-class family, had a very comfortable life and have just got on with planning for a life with a good job, a wife, couple of kids, a comfortable home, an executive car, a few holidays abroad every year and a pension. Since I've met you I've turned all that on its head! Being with you has helped me to understand myself better and I have a more meaningful vision of where I am going in life. I have concentrated on setting myself high personal standards and I've realised that life is really what you make it. My family and friends have said that I've become a better person and that they have seen a change in me since I've been with you. What makes me laugh is that people in this country think being pushy is a bad thing, but you're a really good example of how by being pushy you have managed to capture people's attention and you've bettered your life as a result.

Steve made me realise that the word 'push' actually stood for all the key attributes I display, and that these are the key characteristics that apply to motivational and inspirational people.

P.U.S.H. for a Vision

At some point in our lives we've been asked, 'Where do you see yourself in five years' time?' Some people have no idea how to answer that question, whilst others know exactly what to say because they have a vision of what they want. Having a vision helps you plan and aim for the life you want to lead, and you can measure your success based on how close you are to achieving your vision. Chapter 5 looks at helping you to prepare your Vision Contract and keep it alive.

P.U.S.H. STANDS FOR:

P: Be Proactive

I demonstrate proactive behaviour and language, and I believe this has helped me to succeed. I never wait for opportunities to come to me; I go and find them. This is the key difference between proactive and reactive people. In Chapter 1, I examine proactive language and behaviour, and give you the tools to start using it.

U: Understand Yourself

The key to influencing others is to understand yourself. You need to be aware of your skills and behaviours, your strengths and the areas you need to develop. Chapter 2 looks at the importance of knowing what you do, how you do it and why you do it the way you do. I'll show you how to identify your learning style, making you more effective in different situations. Knowing what your strengths are and how to develop yourself is an opportunity for personal growth, and will certainly give you a head start in life.

S: Sell Yourself

Showing off your skills, attributes and all the ingredients that make you who you are is crucial in our competitive world. We all sell to each other every day; the difference is that some of us do it consciously and some of us unconsciously. Being able to sell your ideas to others confidently and with passion comes from having the right attitude and approach. Chapter 3 will show you the skills that will enhance your selling ability and keep your name at the front of people's minds, even when you are not there.

H: Have High Standards

We British love to live by standards. Living your life to a high standard tells others you are in control of your life. Having high standards in the little things goes a very long way. Take your desk at work for example – is it a complete mess with paper all over it, making it difficult for you to find what you are looking for quickly? Or is it spotless and organised? What does your desk say about your standards? If you were a boss judging the next promotion on the state of two desks, who would you give it to? High standards can't be achieved without having goals in life, and Chapter 4 provides the tools for effective goal-setting.

P.U.S.H. for Your Values

Our values make us unique. They are moulded from our life experiences, such as education, culture, parents' values, where we come from and many other factors. Values help us make decisions, from the kind of milk we buy to who we vote for. Knowing what your values are is another key ingredient to being successful – if you live by your values then you are making decisions about your life based on what makes you happy. Chapter 6 looks at the importance of values in the decision-making process.

P.U.S.H. for Success

Success is whatever you want it to be. For some, it's about being a good parent and having a happy and loving family; for others, it's about living the high life and being able to eat in top restaurants and wear the latest clothes. Success is not the same for everyone, and that's the important message of Chapter 7. Achieving your goals in life is what makes you successful, and it's those goals that define individual success.

ACTION PLANS

At the end of each chapter I have put together an Action Plan. This is to help you record, analyse and monitor your progress in the exercises you are set. Let me tell you one thing now: **DO THE EXERCISES – THEY WORK!** You will not develop by just reading the words. You will develop by **DOING** what the words say.

The Action Plans are meant to be part of your life. **THEY MUST NOT JUST SIT IN THIS BOOK!** You have to lift them from the page and put them in your diary, on your mobile phone, on your computer, on your fridge door – anywhere as long as they are visible and remind you of what you are trying to do.

The Action Plans are designed for you to make them

your own. How hungry you are for success depends on how committed you are to following a process and sticking with it. I was once told, 'Never shortcut the process.' I never did.

The Action Plans will help you get a better understanding of what success means to you. They will give you the time to focus on you and what you want out of your life. They will make you think and help you take steps towards your own development. I have put these action plans together to:

- Keep you focused.
- Test your stamina and commitment to developing yourself.
- Give you a sense of achievement when goals and targets are met.
- Keep you moving forward and setting yourself new goals.
- Keep you motivated and interested in your life.
- Improve your learning skills.
- Open you to new experiences and opportunities.
- Give you a purpose for improving your life.
- Help you make better-informed decisions about your life quickly and more often.
- Make you happy.

HOW TO USE THIS BOOK

There is a lot of information in each chapter. Information should always be digested one bite at a time, otherwise it becomes too much and there is the danger of overload. I highly recommend the following approach:

- Before moving on to each new chapter, practise what you have read.
- After a week, move on to the next chapter, having put your new learning into practice and seen some results.
- Make a habit of doing things the new way – once it's a habit, it will be a part of your life.

This book is not about you trying to be perfect; it's about recognising and realising your own potential to achieve what you want in life. It gives you the tools to carry out your work, life and play with a strong mind and attitude. You are the foundation of your success, and this book will help you build on that foundation.

1

Be Proactive

GOALS FOR THIS CHAPTER:

- ▓ To become confident in yourself.
- ▓ To gain a sense of achievement from doing an activity you've been putting off for a long time.
- ▓ To become a positive person.

Proactive: 'Gaining control by taking the initiative'
OXFORD ENGLISH DICTIONARY

My interpretation of the above definition is getting off your backside and making things happen. It's that simple. I have always been active in seeking out opportunities, knocking down barriers and finding another way when someone says, 'No, you can't do that.'

Is there someone in your life who makes you think, 'I can't believe how successful he/she is'? The reason you can't believe it is because, deep down, you know that you have exactly the same, if not more, skills, qualifications and experience, but somehow you've managed to get in a rut and not move forward.

PROACTIVE VERSUS REACTIVE

What is the difference between successful people and those who are not? The answer is the difference between *proactive* and *reactive* people.

You can spot someone who is proactive just by listening to their language and watching their behaviours. They are usually very positive, forward-thinking people who are always taking advantage of opportunities and are successful in living the life they want. They never seem to take anything for granted and are prepared to work hard to succeed. Proactive people have energy and an excitement about them, and they always seem to be moving ahead.

Reactive people, on the other hand, like to play things safe. They don't like change and working out of their comfort zone. They are happy to let life tick by and see what it throws up. They tend to be creatures of habit and need a lot of persuading to accept new ideas. They like to say 'chill out' and use a lot of excuses to justify their limited achievements in life.

Proactive versus Negative Language

We do some things in our everyday life automatically. We've been doing them for so long that these behaviours define who and what we are. People become used to our habits and so, when we do something different, they tend to say, 'Ooh, that's not like him/her. I wouldn't have expected that. It's really out of character.' The language we use at work, at home and in our social lives says more about who we are, what we represent and where we are going than anything else.

I was once told by my sales manager, 'Saira, you're not the brightest button in the team but I like your attitude and the fact that you're always positive and wanting to do your best, so for this reason you're being promoted to Area Sales Manager for London.'

There were other people in the team who were older, more experienced and certainly more knowledgeable than me. They had two things in common, however: they were always looking for problems rather than solving them; and they were constantly moaning about the amount of work that had to be done rather than getting on with it. What they didn't realise was that every time they were in front of the sales manager, he was judging their approach and attitude from the language they used, as that said more about them than anything else.

That was a very important lesson for me. Until then, I hadn't taken too much notice of my language and the words I used to communicate. When I got a promotion based on my positive character, I became fascinated with language, trying to identify the difference in my language compared to others. I also began to listen very hard to the words people used to describe others, their situations, their experiences and themselves.

What I have discovered over the years is that people fall into two distinct camps: those who use proactive language and those who use reactive language. A lot of people are unaware of which camp they fall into and therefore oblivious of the impact their language has on how they are perceived by other people.

Do You Use Proactive or Reactive Language?

Being able to recognise the difference between proactive and reactive language will help you analyse your own language and that of others around you. The table opposite will give you a good starting point.

Proactive language	Reactive language
I can do that if I try.	I just know I won't be able to do it.
I will be able.	I won't be able. I'm not very capable.
I should be able to lose weight if I control my appetite.	I'll never lose weight. I just can't help myself when I see all that chocolate.
I know why I am upset.	I blame him. He makes me really upset.
I take full responsibility for my actions.	It's not my fault.
I have great skills.	I haven't got any more skills than the next person.

Now that you can see the difference, I'm sure you've already started to think about those people who fall into the proactive camp and those who fall into the reactive camp.

To illustrate the point further, I will now show you how proactive and reactive language is used by people in everyday situations.

Changing Jobs

Everyone finds changing jobs a very big decision. Have you noticed, though, how some people seem to change jobs really easily and get better positions and more pay every time, whereas others seem to stick at one job and move up the career and pay ladder painstakingly slowly?

I have a friend, a computer analyst, who has been with the same company for over 16 years. He's very bright and good at his job, but every time I meet him he moans about how he doesn't find it challenging any more, that he isn't being paid as much as he would like, and that he hasn't been promoted for a long time. When I asked him whether he'd ever considered changing his job, the amount of excuses he came up with was unbelievable. It made me think to myself, 'Well, what's the point of trying to help you get another job when you're not even excited at the thought of it?'

I have become something of an expert when it comes to changing jobs. I've worked as a town planner, a biscuits sales rep, an area sales manager, a national sales manager, an advertising sales rep, and a corporate on-line sales manager. So I've worked in the biscuit industry, the telephone advertising industry, the on-line industry and now the media industry. Some of you might be thinking, 'Blimey, you've jumped around a lot.' Yes, I have, and it's because every time I moved I got more money, a better position and learnt more skills.

So how have I managed to do it? Well, whenever I feel the need to change jobs I take a piece of paper and write down why I want to change and what I need to do to make that change. The words I write down are positive, to give me motivation and a willingness to move forward. The table below shows the language I would use and the language a reactive person would use when considering a job change.

Saira's language	Reactive language
I will look for a better job because I know I can do better and get paid more.	I don't think I can find a better job than I already have.
I want to make sure I have changed jobs within the next three months.	I'm not bothered when I change jobs; it'll happen when it happens.
I am so excited about a new opportunity.	I'm not sure if I am ready for a change.
I want to meet new people and be challenged in a new environment.	I'm so used to working in this team of people now.
I know I need to develop my skills further and I can only do that if I change jobs as I have gone as far as I can in this company.	I'll wait until I get my promotion. I've been here ages; they'll promote me at some stage when they feel I have all the skills.
I will be happy to relocate as long as it's the right job, the right money and a move forward in my career.	If I move jobs, I'll have to move home and I can't be bothered with all that hassle.
I'll ask for some advice about my CV to make sure I'm presenting myself in the best possible way.	I'll just update my CV with some new dates. There's nothing else exciting to add to it.

Asking for a Pay Rise

You're the most dedicated hard worker; you're always the one to help out when things go pear-shaped, and you will take on more tasks to help the team out. So why is it that the pay rise goes to someone else and not you? I'll tell you why: because in your mind you're talking yourself out of it, and the language you use will justify all the reasons not to ask for one. At the end of the day, it's easier not to ask for a pay rise than to ask for one; that way you just don't have to deal with an awkward situation. In your mind you really want someone to come over to you and say, 'I've noticed your hard work and I'd like to give you a pay rise.'

Unfortunately, that is rarely going to happen nowadays. I have found that companies will not shell out money if they don't have to. The culture now is if you don't ask, you don't get. A lot of companies play on the fact that people are too scared to approach managers for a pay rise; they know that people will work for them anyway rather than resign and go through the hassle of looking for another job.

I have never been shy of asking for what I deserve. I know I work hard, that I give 100 per cent effort and am good at what I do. I know that, compared to other people, I contribute more and work outside of my job description. When you go to ask for a pay rise you need to have prepared your evidence so you can demonstrate why you deserve the pay rise.

The other important element is knowing the right time to ask for a rise. All companies differ: some may have set times of the year when they review people's pay; others just do it on an *ad hoc* basis. The table below demonstrates the kind of language I would use to justify a pay rise compared to the language a reactive person would use to talk themselves out of a pay rise.

Saira's language	Reactive language
I have passed my six-month probationary period and will ask for the pay rise I was promised after that period.	I've only been here six months. It's too early to ask for a pay rise.
I have demonstrated a consistently high performance and have achieved all my objectives. I want a pay rise for my efforts and contribution.	My boss tells me that our department is not doing well, so I won't ask for a pay rise.
I am one of the most experienced workers in this company and my pay needs to reflect this.	I am scared that if I ask for a pay rise my boss will hold a grudge against me.
My pay is not motivating me to work harder and I need to tell my boss about this now before I get demotivated.	There are other people who need a pay rise before me as they've been here longer.

Saira's language	Reactive language
I've taken on more responsibility in this role and that needs to be recognised in a pay rise.	Why should I work any harder? I don't get paid enough to work hard.
I will ask for a pay rise because if you don't ask you don't get. I want to know what my manager has to say about it.	I won't ask for a pay rise because I took all my allowed holidays this year.

If you start using proactive language, you'll find that your whole outlook on life changes. You never hear personal trainers in the gym motivating their students by using phrases like, 'You're never going to do it,' 'You're useless,' and 'I'd give up if I were you.' Instead they use positive language like, 'Well done,' 'That was great,' 'That's the best you've done,' 'You can do it.' Think about how your language makes you sound: are you making excuses or positive contributions? Does your language give people the impression you are confident and eager, or that you're scared and weak?

Proactive Behaviour

Just like language, people's behaviours can be categorised as proactive or reactive. On the one hand, there are those people who are willing to have a go, try new things and broaden their experiences to improve their opportunities. On the other hand, you have those who always do what they've been doing and are opposed to trying new ways.

Behaviours, like our language, define who we are and what we represent. The majority of people have very little understanding of how their behaviour impacts other people's perception of them. Being conscious of your behaviour and controlling it is powerful and can help you shape the image you want people to have of you.

Our behaviours can be demonstrated by our attitude, approach and body language. I find it amazing that so many people find it hard to express themselves positively through their behaviour.

When I first started dating my husband Steve, I found it very strange how easily he became distracted by things around him. When I was talking to him about something really meaningful in a busy environment, such as a pub, he'd listen to the first few sentences and then his eyes would wander over my shoulder because something else had caught his attention! This used to drive me mad. I confronted him, telling him I found his behaviour really off-putting and felt he wasn't really interested in me and what I had to say. He was mortified that I felt that way and apologised sincerely. Interestingly, he told me, 'Saira,

I have no idea I'm doing it. I get distracted really easily and find it hard to concentrate when lots of things are going on around me.'

Once he realised his behaviour was upsetting me, he asked me to help him get better at concentrating. We came up with the following solutions:

- When going to a busy place, Steve had to sit with his back to the room so that he could only see me and not the action going on around him.
- Making eye contact was really important, and he'd consciously make sure he was doing that to demonstrate he was concentrating on what I was saying.
- Every time I thought Steve's concentration was drifting, I would just say, 'Hello, are you listening to me?' and he'd regain focus.

I'm pleased to say that I now have a husband who can concentrate on what I'm saying without getting distracted by the leggy blonde who walks into vision – now ladies, that is a result, isn't it! But on a more serious note, Steve feels a lot more confident in himself because he has learnt to control his concentration levels. This has helped him improve the quality of his interactions with people both at home and at work.

Recognising Proactive and Reactive Behaviour

Recognising proactive and reactive behaviour will help you identify your own behaviours as well as those of others. Becoming conscious of your actions and those of others around you will give you insight into how you can become proactive and leave a positive image of yourself in people's minds. The following scenarios will highlight the different approaches and attitudes displayed by proactive and reactive people when dealing with situations.

Proactive behaviour	Reactive behaviour
Makes eye contact	Looks away
Finds solutions	Finds problems
Punctual	Late
Actively listens	Disengaged
Self-aware	Unaware of self and others
Prepares early	Last-minute preparation
Asks for feedback	Accepts failure
Energetic	Lethargic
Sets goals and objectives	Doesn't have any set measures
Takes a risk	Averse to risks
Asks for help	Ignores help

Buying a House

Although this is seen as one of the most stressful things you can do, some people manage to buy a house with very little to moan about. Having a proactive approach and attitude allows you, in some situations, to take advantage of money-saving opportunities. The more open you are to new ideas and ways of doing things, the more opportunities you will create for yourself. There are now many different ways to buy a house, but it's amazing how some people just don't seem to make an effort to find out what's new and how it can help them save time and money and get their ideal home.

Let's take an example. How would the behaviours of a proactive and reactive house-hunter differ? The two key behaviours we all demonstrate when we try something new are our *attitude* and *approach*.

Proactive Attitude: A proactive person looking to buy a new house would certainly set themselves some goals before they even started to look at houses. These guidelines would typically be:

- I want the best deal.
- I don't want a chain.
- I've set a budget which I will not go over.
- I need to be near schools, have a garden, have

good motorway access, have plenty of storage, be in a quiet residential street, be close to local shops and have pleasant neighbours.

Proactive Approach: People with a 'can do' attitude are more likely to achieve what they are looking for than those who can't be bothered. So the approach someone proactive would take to buy their ideal house would be as follows:

- Explore various options to get the best mortgage deal on the market.
- Register with various agencies to find the right house: internet, estate agents, papers, auctions.
- Negotiate solicitor's fee to get a better price.
- Communicate regularly with agencies involved to show them your eagerness for results.
- Talk to neighbours to get a feel for the area before moving in.

Most Likely to Say... At the end of the process the proactive person is likely to say something along the lines of, 'This is the best move and it has everything I'm looking for in a new home.'

How does this compare to a reactive attitude and approach to the same task?

Reactive Attitude: A reactive attitude can be demonstrated by not planning. The reactive person might think, 'I want a house, so let's see what's out there.' This attitude is not helpful because it doesn't specify exactly what kind of house needs to be found. Looking through all the houses in the local paper will be time consuming and will become increasingly irritating and confusing if you don't know what you are looking for.

Reactive Approach: A reactive approach doesn't take charge of the situation but reacts to circumstances, resisting change and new ways of doing things. A reactive approach to buying a house would include the following actions:

- Doesn't write down key criteria and keeps changing their mind about what's important on every visit to a property.
- Sticks with current mortgage provider and doesn't shop around for the best deal.
- Accepts solicitor's fee as quoted and doesn't make an attempt to negotiate and get a bargain.
- Waits for agencies to phone and update them rather than chasing for news and updates.
- Registers with one estate agency and looks in local paper. Doesn't take advantage of the internet

and auctions, which are more innovative ways of buying a house and can be very cost effective.

■ Doesn't talk to neighbours prior to moving in to get an impression of what they are like as sees this as being too intrusive.

Most Likely to Say... A reactive person with such an attitude and approach is likely to say, 'We didn't realise just how much traffic tears down the street during rush hour.'

My experience with reactive people is that they rarely know exactly what type of house or area they want to live in, or how to get a good deal for themselves.

Booking a Holiday

The travel industry has become more competitive than ever. The amount of offers that are available all year round are incredible and the low-cost airlines have made flying overseas accessible to all budgets. The internet has given power to customers to book journeys online and create their own holidays. Holidaymakers now have more choice and control over where they go and what they want to do. Having a proactive attitude and approach can get you the holiday of your dreams without creating a massive hole into your bank balance.

Proactive Attitude: A person with a proactive attitude looking to book a holiday would think along these lines:

- I will ensure that I can get the best deal by being as flexible as I can about when I can go. I want the best holiday at the best price.
- I will try some new places to get a new experience and take advantage of the offers.
- I don't mind if I am not in a five-star hotel as long as the room is comfortable, clean and is close to the amenities that I want.
- I'm quite happy to book last minute to get the best deals.

Proactive Approach: Booking a holiday has to be one of the most pleasant activities to carry out because the images we see of, perhaps, blue skies, golden sands, palm trees and clear aqua seas transport us to where we would rather be all day every day. It's so nice imagining being in the location of your dreams and spending your time exactly as you wish. Let's face it: it beats working, doesn't it? A proactive approach to booking your holiday could be the difference between getting the best or the worst experience of your life. It will require you to invest some good quality time in exploring all the different options available to you and then weighing these up so as to make informed decisions.

A proactive approach would be to:

- Explore the internet, travel agents, newspapers and travel guides, and ask friends for exciting holiday destinations.
- Compare prices on the internet, in travel agents and newspapers to get the best deal and cheapest time to travel.
- Check the possibility of just booking a flight and getting accommodation once you are out there.
- Write down a list of criteria important for the holiday, such as a four-star hotel, all-inclusive package, gym, swimming pool, close to the beach, no kids, evening entertainment.
- Check weather reports for the time you plan to go on holiday.
- Check information on the surrounding area for activities away from the hotel.
- Work out the exchange rate and decide if it's cheaper to buy toiletries out there. This also saves dragging a heavy bag to the airport.

Most Likely to Say... A person who takes a proactive approach to booking their holiday is likely to say, 'I got a four-star hotel in South Africa for the same price as a two-star hotel in the Costa del Sol in peak season.'

Reactive Attitude: I know some people, like Mac and Margaret (my parents-in-law), who are retired and go to the same villa in Majorca every year for a week in the summer. Now, I think that's fine. They go because, for them, it's a safe bet with the weather, they have made some friends and they love the villa. However, I know some young couples who go to the same place every year for no other reason than it's all they know and they don't want to venture into a new environment. This reactive attitude can cost money and valuable life experience.

Reactive Approach: A person who takes a reactive approach to booking their holiday most certainly does not get a bargain. Their actions would be:

- Looks at the new brochure for the same holiday destination as last year because they are scared to try another one.
- Books their holiday through the local travel agent because they don't know how to look for bargains on the internet.
- Goes on holiday at the same time every year because it's a habit.

- Books the same hotel as last year because it's 'tried and tested' and it's 'better to be safe than sorry'.
- The holiday price for the same location and hotel goes up every year, making it an expensive destination for the facilities it provides, but the reactive person still goes ahead and books because they don't want to shop around.
- Buys suntan creams in England at full price because they don't think the foreign stuff is any good, and anyway the instructions would be in a foreign language.

Most Likely to Say... A holiday planned with a reactive approach would lead someone at the end of the holiday to say something like, 'I can't believe how expensive this place has become for the facilities it provides. Those kids really got on my nerves; there seem to be more and more every time I come.'

HOW BEING PROACTIVE HAS HELPED ME SUCCEED

Being proactive is another word for getting off your backside and getting things done. That's what I have had to do because I had no alternative. I wanted to better myself, I wanted to be financially independent and I wanted to enjoy some of the good things that life offers; the only way to get all that was to go for it. I've never really been scared of trying new things, meeting new people or even speaking my mind. To be honest, I thought everybody was like that. However, as I have become more experienced I have realised that not everybody cares for being proactive, or even positive, and that some people seem to dwell on the negative aspects of life and prefer to moan about what could and should have been.

When I realised that it was actually my language, behaviour and attitude that set me apart from other people I began to focus on these aspects and looked for ways to improve myself so that I could be better and more effective in the things that I did. Being proactive has helped me to gain confidence over the years and this in turn has helped me to challenge myself and my environment and move forward in life.

I think my biggest strength is that I never take NO for an answer. If I believe strongly in something and I want it I will find lots of ways to overcome any obstacles that people may throw in my way. I will carry on until I get the result that I am looking for. I think it is this quality that has helped me to be the person that I am today.

I'd like to share with you some of my experiences where I have been proactive and how this has helped me to be successful. You will see that being proactive is not about grand gestures but about applying a 'can do' attitude to everyday activities. I will also share with you the role models in my life who have demonstrated to me that if you want to be successful you really have to get on and do it.

Buying my First Property

I was 24 years old, living in Brighton and working as a chartered town planner with a salary of £11,000 per year. I was living in a small studio flat and desperate to buy my own place. My friends at the time were still living life as students, even though they'd left university three years before; the last thing they wanted to do was to buy a house. I vividly remember a friend of mine saying, 'What do you want to buy a house for? It's so much responsibility and it'll tie you down. You won't have much freedom to do what you want; you won't be able to go travelling or move around. It's so much hassle.'

My mindset was totally different. I was thinking, 'Why am I paying all this rent to someone when I could be paying a mortgage for my own property and have something to show for my money?'

I managed to find a gorgeous one-bedroom flat with

REACTIVE LANGUAGE ☒

PROACTIVE ATTITUDE ☑

a conservatory for £42,000. The only problem was that my sums didn't add up. I wasn't earning enough money to be eligible for a mortgage, and I didn't have enough deposit to put down as security.

Nevertheless, I went to see the bank manager and struck up a really good friendship with her. She helped me with the sums and, after going through all my outgoings and incomings, she could see that I could afford the monthly repayments. However, I still needed to come up with a deposit and proof that my wages would increase.

I had no hesitation in asking my boss if he could write a letter to confirm that he would give me a pay rise in due course, which would demonstrate that I would be able to pay the mortgage. My boss was really great at helping me out and signed the letter for me that the banks wanted; actually, he had no intention of giving me a rise and I knew that it was only to help me get access to a mortgage. The hardest thing I had to do was ask my dad for help. I was really against doing this because I knew he didn't have a lot, and he'd have to dip into his humble savings to help me out. The only way I was happy to take his money was on the basis that I paid back every penny. My father lent me the £4,000 I needed and I bought my first flat.

I paid my father back the £4,000 by sacrificing my

comfort and privacy. I rented out the main bedroom to a friend, and the money I got from this paid the mortgage. With the money I saved, I paid back my father. I slept in the conservatory on a single bed for four years to make ends meet.

Looking back now, I'm so glad that I bought my flat. It was hard work, but deep down I knew it made sense to buy. Even though some of my friends were discouraging and it looked impossible to raise the finance, I still explored the possibility and opened up opportunities for myself. I never once accepted that I couldn't do it. I had to be cheeky in some instances and get people to help me out but I was determined to get what I wanted. At the back of my mind I always thought, 'If I don't try I'm never going to find out.' I still have that flat today, and I can tell you it's worth a lot more than £42,000. The friends who discouraged me all that time ago are still finding it hard to take their first step onto the property ladder.

Applying for *The Apprentice*

I was working as a sales consultant for an on-line recruitment company in London when I heard about *The Apprentice*. The PR girl had sent an email to a few people in the company informing them that the BBC was looking for contestants for a new business reality show. I overheard someone talking about the details and said, 'What email? I haven't received anything.' I went to the PR girl and asked her if she could forward me the application form. She did, adding, 'You'd better be quick because today is the deadline.'

The application form had been sent to about 10 people in my office, and everyone seemed interested in applying. That evening, I went back home and started to read the information about what the show involved. The details were very brief indeed, but the key points were as follows:

- Sir Alan Sugar was looking for an apprentice.
- The salary would be £100,000 per annum to the winner.
- If chosen, you would have to commit to three months of filming in a secret location.
- There would be no contact with family or friends.
- You would have to give up your job to do the filming.

I immediately thought, 'What a great, exciting opportunity to better my job prospects and to work for one of the most colourful entrepreneurs in Britain. Why not? I've got as good a chance as anyone else.'

That night I filled out the very long application form

PROACTIVE ATTITUDE

and managed to get it sent with only seconds to spare before the deadline.

The next morning, I asked all those people who'd received the email whether they'd applied or not. To my amazement, only three out of the ten bothered to fill out the application form and send it off. I remember the excuses that were given by those who didn't fill out the form:

- 'I couldn't be bothered to fill out the long form; they were asking really stupid questions.'
- 'There's no way people like us are going to have a chance. These TV companies just go for people they already know.'
- 'I can't take the risk. What if the boss finds out I'm applying to go on a TV show?'
- 'It's on BBC2 so it won't be a big show.'

It's amazing how different people treat opportunities. When I filled out the application form, all I could think about were the positive aspects of wanting to be on *The Apprentice*: the chance to meet Sir Alan, the possibility of improving my career prospects, the chance to increase my salary and to use the media as a platform to get noticed.

A week later, I was contacted by TalkBack, the production company, inviting me for my first interview.

NEGATIVE LANGUAGE ☒

I was told at the interview that everyone who'd submitted their application form was being seen by the production company, and that candidates would be selected on the basis of interview, rather than on the details of the application form.

The fact that I had bothered to fill out my form and send it off gave me the opportunity of a lifetime. Others in my office had the same opportunity but, due to their reactive attitude and behaviour, let it slip through their fingers.

MY PROACTIVE ROLE MODELS

I have always liked to have role models in my life to motivate and inspire me, and I use them as a benchmark for my own success. They are people that make me think, 'I want to be just like you,' because I admire their get-up-and-go. They focus on getting things done rather than waiting for things to happen. Their life stories are full of events where they pushed themselves outside their comfort zones to experience new opportunities, and then took those opportunities to improve themselves.

1. My Parents

I think I had a head start in life when it came to being proactive, because my parents are the most proactive people I know. In 1965, they were given the opportunity to come to England to work. It meant leaving their home, family and friends in Kashmir and taking a risk in making a more prosperous life in England. Can you imagine that? What would your gut reaction be if someone said to you, 'We hear there's an opportunity in another country to work and make some money, but it will mean leaving your family and friends behind'? They arrived at Heathrow Airport with just £5 in their pockets and set about making a life for themselves.

All I ever saw my parents do was work hard at creating the opportunities to better themselves. They had to face poverty, discrimination and limited opportunities but, despite all this, they improved their life. They never made an excuse for their struggle, and they never had to beg or borrow. Watching my parents build something out of nothing has been proof in my own mind that being proactive brings successful results.

2. My Husband Steve

Steve is an Essex boy. He had a comfortable upbringing with very little to worry about. His parents' expectations were for him to get a local job, marry a local girl and live a comfortable life like theirs had been. Steve, however, has never been satisfied with being comfortable. When he met a German girl at the age of 21, he took the chance of following her to Germany and living there with her. He left his friends, family and boring job behind at a time when people didn't really do that kind of thing. The relationship didn't work out, so he was left in a country where he didn't speak the language and had no job. Returning to the UK was the easy option, but he decided to make a go of it in Germany. He lived in Munich for 18 months, working as a hotel porter, and mastered the language in that time.

Steve met many American business people in the hotel where he was working. He began to think, 'I can be like them. I've got what it takes.' This gave Steve the confidence to consider going to university at the age of 24 as a mature student, to better his job opportunities. He put himself through university and, after graduating, got a sales job at a blue-chip company in London.

He has never looked back. His jobs have taken him all around the world. Now, at the age of 41, he owns three properties and runs his own internet business. His mantra in life is, 'It's never too late and you're never too old.' I think it's a great attitude to have and it's certainly one of the key qualities that attracted me to him.

ACTION PLAN

So now it's your turn to get proactive! But before you start your action plan, I want you to commit to the following four points and say them out loud to yourself:

1. I really want to become more proactive.
2. I will be conscious of my language and behaviour when I am with other people.
3. I will promise myself that I will commit to my Action Plan and not give up.
4. I will review my action plan every morning before going to work or starting my activities.

Tips to Make Your Action Plan Work

Getting proactive is about doing, and an Action Plan will help you visualise what you are doing and keep track of your achievements. Your Action Plan needs be a part of your everyday life. My tips for bringing it alive are as follows:

■ Write down on a separate **Post-it note** each task you need to complete and stick it on your fridge door, your car dashboard, your desk at work – anywhere you'll see it regularly. This will help remind you what you have to do. Once you've completed the task, rip up the note and move on to the next one.

■ **Set an alarm on your phone** that goes off every two hours and reminds you of the following question: 'Are you being proactive?'

■ Set up a reminder on your PC so that **you send yourself an email** every hour which says, 'Have you completed your task yet?'

I need to remind myself of the key goals I am trying to achieve. Otherwise I get distracted and, before you know it, I've not done the things I promised myself I would do. This leaves me feeling demotivated and upset with myself. Reminding yourself makes the exercise more valuable and demonstrates to others that you are really serious about what you are doing. Use a separate piece of paper to write down your answers.

Task 1: Get in Tune with Yourself

To become proactive, you need to be more conscious of your language, behaviour, attitude and approach to life, situations and people.

When you find yourself in a situation that is important to you, ask yourself the following five questions:

1. Am I taking responsibility?
2. Am I being positive?

3. Am I aware of how I am coming across to others?
4. Is my language helping me to create opportunities?
5. How am I behaving?

Now look through the following list and *honestly* tick the ones that are applicable to you:

I am aware of my own behaviour. ✓
I am aware of the behaviour of others. ✓
I am aware of the reactions of others to my behaviour.
I am aware of my reaction to the behaviour of others. ✓
I am aware of how much I talk. ✓
I am aware of how much I support others. ✓
I always explain my disagreements.
I am adventurous.
I am sensitive to the feelings of others. ✓
I am aware of how much I interrupt others. ✓
I am aware of how much I really listen to others. ✓
I tell others what my feelings are. ✓
I am mostly positive. ✓
I am always on time. ✓
I have more than three hobbies in my life that I do regularly. ✓
I exercise three times a week.
I am aware of the language I use. ✓
I always use positive language.

I am described as a positive person.	
I try new things. ✓	
I speak more than one language.	
I take risks in my life.	
I have get-up-and-go.	
I like to plan and prepare before doing a task or an activity.	
I like writing things down. ✓	
I make eye contact when I talk to people. ✓	

Pick out the top three statements that do not apply to you at the moment and write down:

- why you want to focus on these
- how these will help you create opportunities
- what you need to start doing to become more proactive and achieve the behaviours you want
- the people you know who demonstrate the behaviours you are looking to achieve – observe them then copy them in a way that suits your style

Task 2: Get Things Done – Be Proactive

Choose three tasks related to your work, social and personal life, which you have been putting off for some time. Write these tasks in the table below and then start to write down the proactive steps you need to take to complete them.

Task	Where am I now?	Where do I want to be?	What steps do I take to get there?	When do I need to complete this task by?	Whose help/support do I need?	What did I learn about myself during this task?
Work task						
Social task						
Personal task						

Once you have completed your three tasks, use this template to do the next three, and so on. In six months, this will form part of your natural behaviour every time you want to get a task done.

Task 3: Measure Yourself

As you change your language and behaviours, record these changes under the following headings:

- How has changing my behaviour/language/attitude/approach made me feel?
- Has anybody noticed I am being proactive and positive?
- How does it make me feel when I've completed a task I've been putting off?
- Have I created more opportunities for myself by being proactive?
- Am I becoming more confident? What does confidence feel like?

SUMMARY

The only person who can change your language and attitude is YOU. You have the choice and the decision-making powers to make a difference in your life.

Proactive language demonstrates to others that you are a positive person willing to try new experiences.

Having a proactive attitude and approach opens up new opportunities and will give you better personal results.

Proactive behaviour gives you the confidence to work outside your comfort zone more of the time.

Everyone has the ability to be proactive; the first step is to start being aware of your own language and behaviour and then observing others around you.

2

Understand Yourself

GOALS FOR THIS CHAPTER:

■ To gain self-awareness: who you are and why you do things the way you do.

■ To improve your skills.

■ To gain self-confidence.

WHO ARE YOU?

Understanding who you are is a key ingredient for a successful life. What amazes me is that there are so many people out there who have no idea of who they are. Let me ask you a simple question: 'Who are you?' What is your response? I guess the first answer you would give me is your name. But does that really give me an explanation of who you are? Does your name provide *you* with the answer to 'Who am I'?

I remember being asked the same question at a training seminar. I was absolutely gobsmacked because I had no idea how to answer. The feeling that I didn't know how to communicate who I was in the right words made me very uncomfortable.

Over the years, however, I have managed to learn a lot about myself from formal study, training and development, and from meeting lots of different people in a variety of situations and environments. Only through learning have I come to appreciate that you can only understand who you are if you learn about the self, and continue to put the self through learning.

What does 'understand yourself' actually mean? From my learning experiences, it means the following:

- You are in touch with your inner self. You know exactly what makes you tick.
- You know your strengths and areas that need to be developed.
- You are in control of your conscious/unconscious behaviours in different situations.

- You have emotional intelligence.
- You reflect on yourself and learn from different people and experiences.
- You encourage others to give you feedback.

I've come to realise that learning doesn't stop once you leave school or university; it continues throughout life. A huge part of my self-development learning came through working in sales roles. This really helped me understand who I am and why I do the things I do in the manner I do.

WHY LEARN?

- Ninety-five per cent of people think that learning about new things boosts your confidence. (*National Adult Learning Survey*, DfEE, 1998)
- Ninety-two per cent of people think that learning about new things is enjoyable. (*National Adult Learning Survey*, DfEE, 1998)
- Seven in ten adults think that learning can lead to a better quality of life. (*Attitudes to Learning*, Campaign for Learning/MORI, 1996)

We all learn in different ways. Just as an athlete knows how to improve their performance by understanding how their body works, we as individuals can learn better if we know how we like to learn.

If you are anything like me, when someone mentions learning the image that springs to mind is a school desk, teacher, lots of books, listening and writing, and then the dreaded exams to find out if you are a good learner or not. If it wasn't for my father, I would have dropped out of school at 16 – not because I didn't like learning but because I didn't like the learning environment. Throughout my school life, up until the age of 18, I felt I wasn't naturally bright and that I had to work really hard to get average results. I never understood why I found it hard to learn. It really affected my confidence and I didn't contribute very much in class in case what I said was wrong and the others laughed at me. My father had a great influence over the subjects I chose to study because he wanted me to be a doctor. It was only when I failed my chemistry, biology and physics papers that my dad realised I didn't have a chance of qualifying in medicine.

When I went to study for my degree, I found to my complete surprise that I was achieving better exam results and was happier in myself. I had no problem being interactive in class and really looked forward to the lessons. What was it about the learning environment that had changed from school to university? The

fundamental differences that made an impact upon my
ability to learn were as follows:

- I chose to study the subjects I was interested in
  rather than be told what I had to do.
- The lessons were taught in a more informal
  manner with the emphasis on coursework and
  producing my own ideas.
- The lecturers encouraged people to have opinions and ideas, and there were no right or wrong
  answers.
- There were lots of people on my course from
  different backgrounds, with a variety of ages
  and experiences. I loved hearing their different
  points of view.
- I was living away from home in an environment
  where I was allowed to grow up and be myself.
- Learning was fun and I was treated as a grown-
  up rather than a child.
- My lecturers were really approachable and helpful and encouraged me to be myself.

I now know that in order for me to enjoy learning, I
have to have the right learning environment, otherwise
I will either just switch off or not perform to the best of
my ability.

What's Your Learning Style?

Imagine you have been to a DIY store and bought a freestanding pine shelf. You put all the pieces that make up the shelf on the floor. What do you do next? Highlight the action that you would take:

- You open up the instruction manual and read it from cover to cover before attempting to put the shelf together.
- You have a quick flick through the instructions to see if there are any diagrams and then start assembly.
- You don't look at the instructions at all and start assembly.
- You phone your mate who you know is really good at DIY and wait for them to put it together for you.

In this instance I would certainly have a go, and my approach would be the second one – I'd have a quick flick and then start on the job. I don't like reading through loads and loads of instructions. I find them boring. I respond to visual aids like diagrams and pictures. I like my communication to be simple and I like it set out really clearly with lots of bullet points. Once I am given a task, I just want to get on and do it quickly.

My husband, on the other hand, is the total oppo-site of me. He loves to digest information; he would settle down with a cup of tea and the instructions and read the whole lot before even thinking of assembling the shelf. I remember on one holiday in Greece he took *The Lord of the Rings* to read on the beach. The sheer thickness of it put me off immediately, but he plodded through all 400 or so pages without much effort at all. (I opted to watch the film, which was highly entertain-ing, and I managed to get the plot.)

The fact that I know I don't like reading through manuals and that I like 'doing' is an indication of my learning style. Knowing my learning style gives me a greater understanding of who I am, and I can apply this knowledge to get better results for myself.

Being aware of your learning style can benefit you in four key ways:

■ **It helps you understand yourself better and why you do the things you do.** Knowing that I like to get the job done quickly and without too much detail helps me to analyse why I do better at some things than others, and why I seem to enjoy myself in certain situations more than others. As I mentioned earlier, I can now understand why I wasn't very good at exams. Learning lots of different subjects at school through absorbing information from books was really hard work for me. I found myself getting bored easily and not being able to concentrate for long. I loved getting involved physically, so PE was always my favourite subject.

■ **It helps you to explain to others what you like and don't like so that people have a better understanding of your needs.** My husband – a Chelsea fan – was trying to explain how the offside rule works in football. He was getting quite frustrated with me when I kept saying, 'I don't get it!' I told him to draw what he meant, and when I could actually see it I quickly grasped it.

■ **It helps you to identify other people's learning styles, and this gives you power to address their needs.** I buy my husband a big thick book every birthday; my sister gets an audio book and my mother gets a cookery book with lots of pictures. I buy these presents knowing that my husband loves detail, my sister is happier learning by listening and my mother loves visualising information.

■ **It can help you to recognise your own development areas and work on skills that will make you more adaptable.** I need to get better at paying attention to detail: at times my attention span can be very short and my mind wanders. I'm very good at starting something with enthusiasm and passion, but find it difficult to complete some tasks with the same level of energy. To improve on this I have taken to reading at least one of the big four newspapers a day from cover to cover. This has helped to improve my attention span, which means I can be more effective in situations where that skill is required.

The Three Learning Styles

Specific learning styles are used in business to help individuals communicate and present effectively, and managers to train and develop people in the right way. The three learning styles that I think best sum up most people are as follows:

- **Visual** – You like to learn from seeing/reading information.
- **Auditory** – You like to learn from hearing.
- **Touchy-feely** – You like to learn from being hands-on.

Most of us like to use all three styles when learning, but there is one style that you will prefer. So how do you know which style you are?

Visual Learners

I am a strong visual learner. I know that if I am in a meeting I really do prefer to see the information displayed on a screen or flipchart. If I ever have a problem understanding instructions or theory, I always try and get someone to present the information visually so that I can

---

VISUAL LEARNERS

- They like their **information** to be presented in pictures, diagrams or charts.

- When they are **explaining** information, they use phrases such as, 'Now **picture** this', '**Imagine** that', 'You **see**, like this'. They don't like listening for too long.

- When **concentrating**, they can get very distracted by movement or activities going on around them.

- They are very **good at remembering faces** rather than names, and good at remembering places rather than what they are called.

- They like to **meet people face-to-face** so they can see who they are talking to.

- When they are reading **they like to re-create images** in their mind so that they can see what characters, places and objects look like.

- When driving, they like to **see** the map rather than follow written instructions.

- They like watching **television**.

---

see what they are talking about. For me, pictures and diagrams help make sense of information. Knowing I am a visual learner has helped me make the right decisions and choices in so many ways. For example, I know exactly which newspapers I like to buy; I know what I want when I am deciding to enrol on a course or training programme; and I also know how to identify visual learners at work, which helps me to communicate with them effectively. I also let people know what I like so that they can meet my needs. This gives me a higher chance of getting satisfaction more of the time.

Auditory Learners

Auditory learners rely heavily on their hearing sense to help them receive information and learn. They have no problem going into a learning environment where they sit and listen to what is being said. The biggest strength auditory learners have is that they are very good listeners and they learn from listening to other people. My friend Sarah is a great example of an auditory learner. She loves football and listens to Radio Five Live commentary all the time, and gets as much joy from that as she would from watching the game on television. She started to learn French a few years ago, and instead of joining her local evening class, she bought some tapes for the car and listened to them on the way to work. One of the things Sarah hates is going out on a Saturday night and ending up in a noisy bar or disco because she can't hear what people are saying and finds it difficult to chat and make conversation. When I meet Sarah, I always make sure we go to a quiet coffee shop so she doesn't get distracted by background noise.

AUDITORY LEARNERS

■ They like to **hear** information.

■ They are **good listeners** and use words such as, 'Do you **hear** what I am saying?', '**Tune** your mind into this', '**Think** about what I am saying'.

■ They get very **distracted by sounds and noises**. They prefer to concentrate in a quiet environment.

■ They are very good at remembering **names** rather than faces. They have a good memory.

■ They **like talking on the phone** rather than meeting face-to-face.

■ They like **listening to the radio**.

■ They like to chat, make **conversation** and listen to others.

'Touchy-feely' Learners

Touchy-feely learners are easy to spot. They love learning by actually doing. Normally, they are very active and energetic people who like to jump in and have a go. They like to touch and feel to make sense of information and the world they live in.

My brother Tariq is a very touchy-feely learner. He is very practical and just loves to work things out. He is a very good painter and decorator, and he's picked up these skills just by having a go – he has never had any training. He started off by painting his own little room whilst living at home. I remember he'd get a bit stuck along the way but he'd manage to work out how to do it rather than refer to a DIY manual. He's also got a great sense of direction, and he'd rather get lost a few times than open up a map! He's a good sportsman too, and you'll often find him either on a football pitch tackling the

'TOUCHY-FEELY' LEARNERS

- They will use words like 'feel', 'touch' and 'hold' when trying to explain information.
- They can get very distracted by activity around them.
- They are good at recording what you did together and will remember past experiences based on this.
- They like to engage in activities.
- They tend to jump right in and have a go rather than reading about it.
- They like to work things out as they go along rather than being told what to do.
- They'd rather watch an action-packed film than read an action-packed book.

opposition or on a cricket pitch with a bat in his hand. He's not an armchair sportsman.

Understanding your own learning style helps you to answer part of the question, 'Who am I? The question-naire at the end of this chapter (page 82) will help you find out exactly which learning style – or styles – you prefer.

LEARNING FROM OTHERS

Feedback

I am quite a stubborn person. There are times when I think I know it all and I'll go ahead and do the things I want to do without much involvement from others. I have a very strong gut reaction, and for most of my life it has served me very well. However, there have been some crucial times when it has gone horribly wrong. For the most part it's because I didn't take the advice I was given or listen to what people were telling me.

When I was younger, from about the ages of 18 to 30, I was reluctant to accept feedback from others. I never took it on board because I always took the feedback so personally as I saw it as a criticism of me. If the feedback was about how I could do better, I'd immediately argue back, explaining why I couldn't do better, listing all the obstacles I faced, and making every excuse under the sun. I took negative feedback as an attack on me. It would take me a long time to recover, and I would find it hard to like the person who had given it to me.

My husband Steve was the first person to bring home the fact that I was very bad at handling feedback. As soon as he mentioned the subject, I remember my body tightening up and immediately blurting out, 'No, I'm not, I can handle feedback.' He just stared at me to reinforce what he'd said. Steve has had a lot of people-management training, and so with his trained eye he could easily spot my problem. The most important things I learnt from Steve about feedback were:

- You can provide feedback to others without upsetting them.
- Feedback should help the individual become more effective.
- You should always ask to be given feedback and be prepared for it, both good and bad.

Providing Feedback without Upsetting People

Has there ever been a person in your life who always tells you what you should do, how you should do it, why you should do it and what you're doing wrong? Does this person's advice get on your nerves? Do their words make you feel negative and demotivated? Do you feel they're always having a go at you?

Well, let me tell you, I did have a person like that in my life. It was my dad. Don't get me wrong: I loved my dad very much and he was a man of great values and standards. When I was growing up, however, I felt there were times when instead of giving me encouragement to do better he'd make me feel I was never good enough. I felt his feedback was always an attack on me; I took it really personally and it would hurt a lot. It was always, 'Saira, you are doing that wrong... The reason you didn't get an A is because you didn't work hard enough... You can't do that because you're a girl.'

I began to associate my dad's feedback as a long list of all the things that were negative about me. After a while I remember switching off and not paying very much attention because I'd heard it all before.

Helping the Individual Become More Effective

The whole point of feedback is to help the individual become more effective and get better results. My father could have improved his feedback to me by:

- Describing the effect of my actions upon the situation.

- Providing me with examples of where I was going wrong.
- Helping me to come up with some alternatives to try.

For example, when I didn't get an A grade, the feedback my dad should have given me is:

Dad: How does it make you feel that you didn't get an A?

Saira: Crap.

Dad: Why do you think you didn't get an A?

Saira: I don't know.

Dad: Do you think you gave yourself enough time to study?

Saira: No.

Dad: What would you recommend for next time?

Saira: That I start to revise earlier.

Dad: Okay, when are your next exams? We'll mark a date in the calendar to make sure you start your revision at the right time and I'll remind you. Will that help you?

Saira: Yes, thanks Dad.

The above would have had a much more positive effect than 'You didn't get an A because you didn't work hard enough.'

Ask for Feedback and be Prepared for it

When you've carried out an activity for the first time, do you like to ask others' opinions on your effort or do you dread their comments? I used to feel the latter, but now I have no hesitation in asking for people's comments and opinions. The fact is that now I know how to give feedback, I also know how to receive it. The most important thing I remind myself is not to take it personally. People are entitled to their opinions and views, and I have to get used to that if I am to learn and take myself forward in life.

KEY TIPS FOR FEEDBACK

When giving feedback:

- Describe the situation, not the person.
- Describe the effect.
- Be positive.
- Provide alternatives.

When receiving feedback:

- Never take it personally; prepare yourself for it.
- Listen and think about it. Does it make sense to you?
- Ask for feedback from people you trust and respect.
- Act upon the feedback to gain the benefit from others' experiences.

Once you can do that, dealing with feedback allows you to learn from other people. That is a very powerful position to be in. I am now in a situation where I ask for feedback all the time. When I had to give a very important speech to some senior executives and directors, I took my husband along for feedback. I asked him, 'How did I come across? Was I too rushed? Did I take too long? How could I have improved it?'

Steve's feedback was honest and factual and it helped me to polish up some of my presentation skills for the next time.

Observation

It's hard to believe that one of the most important ways to learn from others is to observe them. I am sure a lot of people do it all the time without realising it.

How many of us love 'people watching'? I do, and I could sit for hours on a sunny day in a coffee shop watching people go by. I did it with a friend once and it was fascinating. I learnt more about what she liked and disliked in that time than ever before. We'd see a woman walk by and our comments would be, 'Oh, I love her coat... She's got a funny walk... Don't like her shoes... Her hair would be better darker than blonde... She's got too much make-up on... Love her handbag...

I think she's a secretary... I bet she's married, no I can't see the ring on her finger...'

By observing others, I have learnt how to conduct myself in a more professional way. The most professional person I know is my husband Steve. I think one of the key reasons I fell in love with him is because he displays many qualities I really admire but don't naturally have myself. Having observed Steve over the years in both working and social environments, I have to admit that he has been a great person for me to learn from. I try to practise the way he does things. Since I have been with him, I know I am a better person than I was before I met him. From observing him I have become better at time management; I listen more; I am less bitchy and I have an open mind about trying new activities.

Similarly, he's learnt from me how to be more daring in life; to appreciate other cultures; and to break away from pleasing other people too much.

By observing others, I feel you can learn how you want to be and how you don't. I bet you can remember instantly all the people you've seen over the years and thought, 'Shoot me if I ever get like that.' I went to a restaurant once for a quiet, romantic dinner with Steve. A woman across the room was being really loud and annoying. I commented on her behaviour and the fact that she couldn't see she was disturbing others. Steve looked at me and said, 'That's like the pot calling the kettle black.' I couldn't believe he thought I was like that woman. But then, having observed her some more, it made me cringe because there had been times when I'd been too loud and my behaviour probably pissed other people off. Having seen what an idiot this woman was making of herself, I have since made sure I don't make the same mistake.

PEOPLE SKILLS

Have you been described as a people person? Do you have a lot of friends? Are you popular? Do you find that when someone has a problem they'd rather talk to you than somebody else?

If you answered yes to all the above, then you are a people person. If you answered no, it explains that you are lacking in some skills, and this is preventing people from engaging with you.

I've been told that I am a people person. To be honest, I was never really sure what it meant. But then I started to observe myself with people and compare myself to others, and it became really obvious why people responded to me in a more positive way.

To me, people are the most important things on the

planet. If you can't communicate with people then I think it's really sad. I get so annoyed at people who send each other emails because they can't be bothered to talk face-to-face, and it really gets under my skin when someone has got something important to say but is too shy to say it. The modern way of life is destroying basic human skills.

In order to learn successfully from other people there are certain skills you have to develop. These skills are so basic and crucial that many people just don't pay any attention to them at all. They are skills that help us engage with people and bring out the best in them, enabling us to understand them better. I have met so many pleasant people whose lack of people skills lets them down. Have you ever met the following types?

- People who have no perception of how they come across to others.
- People who only talk about themselves.
- People who don't listen to what you have to say.
- People who rarely ask questions of others.
- People who can't sympathise with your situation.

I have identified the abilities to 'listen' and to 'question' as being crucial to developing excellent people skills:

Listening

Are you a good listener? I used to be a really bad listener. My worst habit was that I'd interrupt before the other person had finished what they were saying. At work we were asked to write down three things about our colleagues' behaviour that we felt could be improved to make them more effective managers. I remember the people in my team felt unanimously that I should improve my listening skills as I interrupted before people finished talking and did not always take in what people were actually saying.

It was only when the matter was brought to my attention that I realised I did have a very bad habit of butting in and that most of the time, when I had asked someone a question, I didn't listen to the answer because I was too busy thinking about the next question I wanted to ask. People gave me the feedback that my behaviour would make them feel I wasn't listening and I didn't care. I felt bad because that's not the impression I wanted to give.

I do find it hard to listen because I'm a person who just wants to get things done, and sometimes I get carried away with my own ideas and forget to involve others. But I have developed my listening skills. By being aware that I am not a good listener I am always conscious when I meet people that I have to let them finish what they are saying. Sometimes in my mind I say, 'Don't interrupt, let them finish.'

The amazing thing is that as soon as I realised I was not a good listener, I also identified others around me who weren't good at listening. As I began to develop myself, it became apparent that there were some who just carried on being bad listeners and didn't want to change.

Listening to what someone is saying requires concentration and it is not as easy as people may think. Listening is about picking up on all the right information and responding accordingly. The most important goal that you need to set yourself when improving your listening skills is to identify exactly what it is you should be listening out for, otherwise you will have no reference point as to which information is important to you and which is not.

Here are the key areas I suggest you should listen out for to be effective:

- Listen for the main idea – identify the overall idea expressed by the person.
- Listen for specific information.
- Infer meaning – listen to identify the difference between what the speaker says and what they actually mean.
- Identify emotion – listen to identify the mood of certain speakers.

- Listen for opinions – listen to identify the attitude of certain speakers.
- Infer relationships – listen to identify who the people are and what the relationship is between them.
- Recognising context – listen to identify the speaker's context.

THE KEY TO GOOD LISTENING

It is also essential that you demonstrate good listening body language. I have found the following tips have helped me to become a better listener:

- Make good eye contact when someone is talking as it shows you are engaged in what they are saying.
- Let people finish what they are saying before butting in.
- If you are in a classroom situation, demonstrate you are listening by taking notes.
- Nod your head to demonstrate to the speaker that you are hearing what is being said.

Becoming a better listener has helped me to be a better manager, wife, sister and friend and it's amazing what you can actually learn if you do truly listen.

Questioning

People who ask questions learn. That's what I have come to believe. I'm always asking questions: trying to find out customers' needs; how people feel; what they think about a certain topic; asking them to explain something to me that I don't understand.

I've never really been backward in coming forward, and I think that has helped me a lot in life. My father used to encourage debates at home. I remember challenging him all the time about the role of women and why Asian women in particular were always the ones cleaning, cooking and covering themselves up whilst the boys could do whatever they wanted. It felt so wrong to me, and I was always trying to find the answers to my questions.

I've also been told that I am really good at bringing people out of their shells. A friend of mine said that her boyfriend's mate was hard work as he never really said anything. I ended up meeting this guy at a party and found that I got on with him really well and we had a real laugh. I found out that he was into indie music and had always wanted to be a DJ. He'd done a stint in Ibiza but went off the idea when he wasn't getting the money he wanted from the effort he was putting in. Now he wanted to be an actor and was looking to join an amateur dramatics society. My friend was amazed at how this guy had opened up to me. 'How did you manage that?' she said. 'I asked,' I replied.

I am amazed at how many people like to talk but don't ask questions. How the hell can you learn if you don't ask questions?

There is an art to this. You need to think about the questions to ask, depending on the outcome you want. Here are some really good tips:

- **If you want people to talk about themselves and give you details** ask questions that begin with: 'who', 'what', 'when', 'why', 'how', 'which'.

- **To get people to be really precise** use words like 'exactly', 'specifically' and 'which' in your questions.

- **To control a person's response and stop them from rambling** ask questions such as: 'Can you give me three good reasons...?'; 'In one sentence can you describe...?'; 'How would you describe yourself in four words?'

- **To clarify information** you can ask: 'Could you clarify that for me...?'; 'What do you mean when you say...?'; 'Am I right in saying that...?'

- **To get a quick yes or no response** use the word 'Do' in your question: 'Do you like this?'; 'Did you watch that last night?'

Next time you are in a social situation, look around and watch who constantly speaks about themselves and who is actually asking the questions. I used to practise my questioning skills by making sure that I found out at least five things about a person that I didn't know. Questioning skills are developed only by asking questions and my tips for getting better are:

- Ask yourself, 'Do I ask enough questions of other people, or do I just talk about myself all the time?'
- Observe your behaviour and be conscious of yourself when you are with other people. Always try and imagine how you come across. If you are talking all the time what impression does that give to the other person? If you ask questions what does that say about you?
- Get to know the different types of questions, i.e. open, closed, probing, and learn how to use these in different situations.

It takes a long time to perfect questioning skills. You have to be very aware of yourself when you are asking questions so you can analyse the response and work out if your question was the right one.

As already stated the simplest way to learn good questioning techniques is to ask questions; it's as simple as that. There's no scientific theory behind it; you just have to make the effort and be interested in people.

I have seen so many managers who are really bad at managing people. The key complaints people have of them are: 'They never listen or ask me how I'm doing or feeling.'

Having an interest in other people has certainly created some amazing opportunities for me. When I have taken the time to find out about a person, I can immediately sense that they feel relaxed and open up, and the conversation becomes more meaningful and engrossing. I also think that asking questions of other people lets them know you are interested in them and that you are not a selfish person who likes the sound of your own voice.

SELF-DEVELOPMENT

You can never do too much in life and you can certainly never develop yourself too much. Up until the age of 30, I can honestly say that I wasn't an extraordinary person. My life consisted of working, going to the gym, enjoying a few package holidays, shopping, watching television and films and going out to eat in nice restaurants. I'd managed to get myself into a comfortable routine.

Have you ever met someone new and thought: 'Wow, you're amazing, you've done so much, you're really interesting. I wish I could be like that'? Well, I had one of those moments and it really made me buck up my ideas.

A group of my university friends got together for a reunion after five years. It was great. Apart from checking out who'd put on weight and who'd lost weight, we all dived in and starting talking about our lives and what we were up to. Well, as I listened to their stories of how they'd gone travelling round the world and learnt to dive and climb mountains, met people from different cultures, and experienced amazing countries, food and traditions, I began to sink into my chair. I felt like a real bore. The only thing I could talk about was my job and the fact that I owned a property. Big deal!

I left that reunion feeling really angry with myself. I was so disappointed that in five years my friends had developed themselves into interesting, exciting and well-rounded people, whilst all I had done was concentrate on getting a better promotion at work. Now don't get me wrong – putting the effort into my work has paid off for me but developing yourself is just as important.

Have you met people who make you think, 'Oh my God, I can't believe how out of touch they are. They're so old-fashioned!'? Well, I think the key reason people become like that is because they stop developing their brains, interests and activities. Life does move at a fast pace, and if you don't keep up it really can leave you behind.

Being an involved person with hobbies and interests gives you a head start in life. You're more likely to create opportunities for yourself and find that you can relate to a wider variety of people.

What does developing yourself mean? It's simple. It means engaging in activities that give you extra dimensions, making you more interesting and also more useful in various facets of life. Your personal development says a lot about who you are and what you stand for. It's a personal statement to others which says 'I am more than just a mother, wife, worker, Asian woman, etc.'

The biggest excuse for people to stop developing themselves is, 'Oh, I don't have time.' The truth is they can't be bothered. Developing yourself can be as simple as:

- reading a book
- finding a hobby
- joining a local sports group

- learning a new skill: cooking, languages, IT, driving
- travelling
- listening to music
- meeting people from different cultures and religions
- doing a course

I haven't met many successful people who don't develop themselves beyond work.

SAIRA'S EXPERIENCE

It has taken me a long time to change my ingrained habits, behaviours and language. Understanding myself has helped me to recognise that I can change and enhance myself to become more effective in my professional and personal life. I used to say, 'I am who I am because I was born that way. I can't change that!' I don't believe that nonsense any more. I believe that I am in control of who I am and if I want to change then I can. I have come to appreciate that change doesn't happen overnight and that it's hard and can sometimes be painful, but it can happen if you want it to. I think the most important thing that I have taught myself is the power of self-awareness. This means that I am in tune with both my mental and physical self. I know myself so well that it's very easy for me to know what is best for me. I can make good decisions based on my 'gut reaction' because I have very strong feelings about what I like and what I don't. I have spent a lot of time getting to know myself. I have pushed myself mentally and physically to understand and appreciate my strengths and limitations. I believe that it is only when you can understand who you are that you can go out and understand others.

So what's my response now when someone asks me 'Who is Saira Khan?' Well, I can say that I am a visual learner. I know which learning situations I like and which ones I would avoid. From gaining other people's feedback and observing myself, I know my strengths and areas to develop.

Strengths	Development areas
I am confident	I can be aggressive
I am proactive	I can be emotional
I am passionate	I can be overbearing
I am of Asian heritage	I can hold grudges
I am energetic	I am not always punctual
I am generous	I can be too opinionated
I am informed	I can rub people up the wrong way
I am fit	I can judge people too quickly
I am open-minded	
I don't moan often	
I have high life standards	
I like to have a go	
I love learning and new experiences	

One of the most important and life-changing experiences I have put myself through was to give up my job at the peak of my career and go backpacking around Southeast Asia. I was 32 years old and just couldn't bear the fact that all I had to show for my existence was a good job. I needed to develop myself and become more worldly-wise.

I decided to go by myself; my family and friends could not believe it. To be honest, I was pretty scared myself, but I needed to prove to myself that I could do it. So in 2002 I waved goodbye to England and arrived back after exactly 12 months, having accomplished the following:

- Travelled to 15 countries by myself.
- Arranged all my own accommodation and travel.
- Qualified as a scuba diver and carried out 15 dives around Asia.
- Did a bungee jump.
- Hiked in various rainforests in the world.
- Saw orang-utans and other amazing wildlife.
- Met tribes and local people and participated in their traditions and customs.
- Saw some of the amazing World Heritage Sites such as Angor Watt in Cambodia.
- Travelled around with people from various parts

of the world, which helped me break down stereotypes of people and their cultures and become more open-minded.

- Spent lots of time on my own, thinking about my life and what I wanted from it.
- Learnt that there are lots of people who have very little in life but manage to smile and keep going.
- Realised how privileged I am to live in a country like England.
- Made me independent.
- Made me realise the importance of family and friends.

What I experienced during that year gave me so much confidence that I really feel I can do anything if I put my mind to it. Travelling really did challenge my mental and physical strength. Living in basic conditions and making an effort with people all the time can be hard work, but the rewards I gained from that experience have developed me into a new person. I think I've become more caring and certainly more interesting. I feel I've got a lot more to contribute in conversations. People say, 'Wow, I can't believe you did that all on your own,' which makes me feel really special. People say you can't change. I say you absolutely can if you want to.

ACTION PLAN

See Chapter 1 for tips on getting the most out of these tasks. Use a separate piece of paper to write your answers to the questions.

Task 1: Discover Your Learning Style

Use the following questionnaire to assess your preferred learning style or styles. Score each statement and then add the totals for each column to reveal the learning style most suited to you. Your learning style is also a reflection of the type of person you are – how you perceive things and the way you relate to the world. This questionnaire helps you to improve your understanding of yourself and your strengths. There are no right or wrong answers.

There are two scoring systems. Choose the one that best suits your purposes:

Method 1 is the simplest and quickest. Select one statement from each line and add the total selections for each column (mostly As, Bs or Cs). The total will indicate your learning-style preference and mix.

Method 2 is a more subtle measurement that takes longer, but is probably worth it. Score each option either 1, 2 or 3 points:

1 = Weakest statement – No, this is not my behaviour.

2 = Neutral statement – I have some tendency towards this behaviour.

3 = Strongest statement – Yes, this is my behaviour.

Give each option a score and then add up the score for each column at the end. This will give you your preferred learning style, but you will also be able to see which style you dip in to, and the style in which you are weakest. This option provides you with a focus to develop your weaker styles.

1. When operating new equipment for the first time I prefer to

A) read the instructions

B) listen to or ask for an explanation

C) have a go and learn by 'trial and error'

2. When seeking travel directions I

A) look at a map

B) ask for spoken directions

C) follow my nose or maybe use a compass

3. When cooking a new dish I

A) follow a recipe

B) call a friend for advice

C) follow my instincts, tasting as I cook

4. To teach someone something I

A) write instructions

B) explain verbally

C) demonstrate and let them have a go

5. I tend to say

A) 'I see what you mean'

B) 'I hear what you are saying'

C) 'I know how you feel'

6. I tend to say

A) 'Show me'

B) 'Tell me'

C) 'Let me try'

7. I tend to say

A) 'Watch how I do it'

B) 'Listen to me explain'

C) 'You have a go'

8. When complaining about faulty goods I tend to

A) write a letter

B) phone

C)   go back to the store, or send the faulty item to the head office

9. I prefer these leisure activities

A)   museums or galleries

B)   music or conversation

C)   physical activities or making things

10. When shopping, I generally tend to

A)   look and decide

B)   discuss with shop staff

C)   try on, handle or test

11. When choosing a holiday I

A)   read the brochures

B)   listen to recommendations

C)   imagine the experience

12. When choosing a new car I

A)   read the reviews

B)   discuss with friends

C)   test-drive what I fancy

13. When learning a new skill I

A)   watch what the teacher is doing

B) talk through with the teacher exactly what I am supposed to do

C) like to give it a try and work it out as I go along by doing it

14. When choosing from a restaurant menu I
   A) imagine what the food will look like
   B) talk through the options in my head
   C) imagine what the food will taste like

15. When listening to a band I
   A) sing along to the lyrics (in my head or out loud!)
   B) listen to the lyrics and the beat
   C) move in time with the music

16. When concentrating I
   A) focus on the words or pictures in front of me
   B) discuss the problem and possible solutions in my head
   C) move around a lot, fiddle with pens and pencils and touch unrelated things

17. I remember things best by
   A) writing notes or keeping printed details
   B) saying them aloud or repeating words and key points in my head

C) doing and practising the activity, or imagining it being done

18. My first memory is of
A) Looking at something
B) Being spoken to
C) Doing something

19. When anxious, I
A) visualise the worst-case scenario
B) talk over in my head what worries me most
C) can't sit still, fiddle and move around constantly

20. I feel especially connected to others because of
A) how they look
B) what they say to me
C) how they make me feel

21. When I revise for an exam, I
A) write lots of revision notes (using lots of colours)
B) talk over my notes, to myself or to other people
C) imagine the information on the revision notes in my mind

22. When explaining something to someone, I tend to
A) show them what I mean

B) explain to them in different ways until they understand

C) encourage them to try and talk them through the idea as they try

23. My main interests are
A) photography, watching films or people-watching
B) listening to music, listening to the radio or talking to friends
C) physical/sports activities or fine wines, fine foods or dancing

24. Most of my free time is spent
A) watching television
B) talking to friends
C) doing physical activity or making things

25. When I first contact a new person I
A) arrange a face-to-face meeting
B) talk to them on the telephone
C) try to get together to share an activity

26. I first notice how people
A) look and dress
B) sound and speak
C) stand and move

27. If I am very angry I

  A) keep replaying in my mind what it is that has upset me

  B) shout lots and tell people how I feel

  C) stomp about, slam doors and throw things

28. I find it easiest to remember

  A) faces

  B) names

  C) things I have done

29. I think I can tell when someone is lying because

  A) they avoid looking at me

  B) their voice changes

  C) I get certain vibes from them

30. When I'm meeting an old friend

  A) I say 'It's great to see you!'

  B) I say 'It's great to hear your voice!'

  C) I give them a hug or a handshake

Total As   _____

Total Bs   _____

Total Cs   _____

Scoring Yourself

- If you scored mostly 'A' then you have a strong preference for visual learning.
- If you scored mostly 'B' then you have a strong preference for auditory learning.
- If you scored mostly 'C' then you have a strong preference for being a touchy-feely learner.

Remember

However you calculate the totals, ensure you use the chosen method consistently throughout the questionnaire.

The total scores for each style indicate your relative preferred learning style or styles.

There are no right or wrong answers. Some people have very strong preferences, even to the extent that they have little or no preference in one or two of the styles. Other people have more evenly balanced preferences, with no particularly strong style.

The point is simply to try to understand as much as you can about yourself and your strengths (your preferred style or styles), and then make best use of learning methods that suit your strengths.

Task 2: Self-awareness

This exercise will help you become better at self-awareness and improve your awareness of others around

	Style	What is this person's preferred method of communication: phone, email, meeting, text?	What do I need to change about my style when dealing with this person?	What does this person need to do to improve their learning style?	What have I learnt about myself?
Partner					
Mum/Mother-in-law					
Dad/Father-in-law					
Sister/Brother					
Son/Daughter					
Best Friend					
Boss					
Colleague					

you. Starting with your own family and friends, begin to observe their behaviours, language, attitude and approach. Write down what you observe about them. Over time, you will see certain patterns emerging for each person; you will be able to get a better understanding of how they operate, and what they like and don't like.

Most importantly, you will get a better understanding of yourself and how you need to interact effectively with each person. Where your communication has been strained with a certain person, you will find that this observation exercise will help you ease the strain.

Task 3: Do Something Different

The most important factor in developing yourself is doing something different. It's about meeting new people, trying a new hobby, reading a different kind of book, learning a new language or even watching a television programme you wouldn't normally watch. Doing something new should educate you in some way; it should give you a new skill; it should give you a different perspective; and you should learn from the experience. You can only develop yourself if you are prepared to work outside your comfort zone. The table below is an example of how you can set yourself tasks and measure how you're getting on. In six months you

	What do I do now?	What do I need to do to improve?	Six-month review: what am I doing now?
Current Affairs	Read the *Sun* newspaper	Listen to Radio 4 news	
	Listen to local radio news	Watch Channel 4 News	
		Buy a broadsheet or read it online	
World Affairs	Watch the news and read papers	Subscribe to *National Geographic*	
		Read *The Economist*	
Television	Only watch soaps, makeover programmes and comedies	Watch documentaries and factual programmes like *Panorama*	
Arts	Never go to a museum or visit the theatre	Go to a local comedy night	
		Visit a museum or an art gallery	
Music	Only watch *Top of the Pops* and listen to Radio 1	Listen to more varied music like classical, jazz, blues	
Literature	Only read popular fiction	Read some biographies and classics	
Technology	Not interested in technology and gadgets	Learn how to email and use the internet	
		Find out about iPods and learn how to download music	
		Learn how to use a digital camera and download photos	
Languages	Only speak one language	Learn to speak French	
Food and Drink	Don't like foreign food	Try new ingredients or style of cooking by eating in new restaurants or getting a takeaway like French, Italian, Indian or Thai	
Social Group	My friends are all of the same class, religion and colour	Try out new activities which will help me make new friends from different backgrounds	

should review yourself and see how far you've developed and how that makes you feel.

SUMMARY

- Commit to learning something new and stick with it.
- Know your learning style – this will help you to understand yourself and others.
- Practise giving and receiving feedback – this will help you to improve yourself and your skills, thereby opening up more opportunities.
- Practise your listening and questioning skills – this will help you to deal with all sorts of people in varied situations.

3
Sell Yourself

GOALS FOR THIS CHAPTER:

- ■ To become confident.
- ■ To open yourself to new opportunities.
- ■ To succeed in achieving your goals.

WHY SELL?

I hear people all the time ranting on about how they'd hate to work in sales and how they're not salespeople. Well, I have to tell you that we are all salespeople. The difference is that some of us are really good at it and some of us are hopeless. That time you went out on a date – you were selling; that time you had an interview – you were selling; that time you decided you wanted a new kitchen and had to convince your husband it was the right thing to do – you were selling; that time you went out with the girls for a drink and put your best dress on to get noticed – you were selling.

Selling yourself will at times also involve negotiating with people to ensure that an amicable decision is reached for all people involved. There are some people out there who have spent weeks attending negotiating training workshops and who have read books on the art of negotiating but still seem to get nervous or perplexed when it comes to asking for what they want. My take on it is this: if you can sell you can negotiate. Negotiation requires exactly the same skills as selling and really the person who normally gets what they want out of the negotiation is the one that has done a better selling job. To be a good negotiator you have to influence, persuade and convince the other person that whatever you are selling – be it an idea, product or a service – is something that they need or want, is of value to them and can bring benefit to them, and that you are the best person to deliver. You need to demonstrate that you are willing to be flexible in order for the sale to proceed. This means that you sometimes have to compromise or meet people halfway to make things happen.

We sell ourselves to others every day. Some people do it without realising; others know exactly what they're doing and the outcome they desire. Take your mind back to the last time you thought to yourself, 'Why doesn't anybody ask me out for a date?', 'Why don't I ever get a lucky break?', 'Why don't I ever get picked at work to do special projects?', 'Why does my husband/wife think I'm ordinary and not extraordinary?', 'Why do I always blend into the crowd?', 'Why does my partner think I don't have anything useful to contribute to debates?' I'll tell you why – because you're not selling yourself; you're not making the most of who you are and who you could be; you're not having a go and you're not confident. Finally, and most importantly, you probably haven't been encouraged to show off because showing off is frowned upon in British culture. I want to tell you that you have something unique to sell about yourself. I believe that everybody has a quality they should be proud of and shout about and use to help themselves get what they want in life; you just need to know how.

The advantages of knowing how to sell yourself are:

- ■ You learn to put yourself first because if you don't, nobody else will.

- You stand out in a crowd of competitive and similar people.
- You demonstrate your confidence to others.
- You create opportunities for yourself.

DIFFERENT SELLING STYLES

Why is it that in one culture being confident and cheeky is celebrated and in another it's frowned upon? It has taken me a long time to understand that your cultural upbringing has a significant impact upon the way you see yourself and how others see you. In my Asian culture, talking loudly, touching and invading personal space is not an issue. Being nosy about people's jobs and how much they get paid is part of getting to know someone. But these characteristics are not very British, and there have been many occasions where British people have described me as 'loud, in-your-face, overconfident and pushy'. I have found it difficult to be myself sometimes, especially when being judged by British cultural behaviours.

So how do you deal with this dilemma? How can you be yourself and appeal to various people and cultures? Well, my advice is to be yourself but at the same time learn to be adaptable and flexible and to understand different cultural practices so that you can be effective in lots of different environments. Many people have commented that my style is very American, and it was only when I visited America and met Americans that I began to understand why.

My view of Americans will be subject to generalisa-tions, but the key things that strike me about them are their confidence, friendliness and their real can-do atti-tude. They don't seem to mind if you've failed in a task or an objective; they celebrate the fact that at least you had a go, and perhaps next time you might do better because you've got experience of how not to do it. In their business approach I think Americans are certainly direct, assertive and competitive in getting what they want. They love winning, like to take a risk and really celebrate successful people. I believe they have some of the best salespeople in the world, and I've experienced this on more than one occasion. When I'm in America I love to go shopping. My intention is to purchase only what I want, but I always manage to come out with more. The salespeople are excellent; they come up to you, they smile, they give you time and attention and chat as if they've known you all their life. They make an effort, bending over backwards to make sure you've had good service. I feel the American culture gives you the opportunity to do well as long as you have the drive, ambition and right attitude.

Compared to the Americans we British have a very different outlook, approach and attitude to life. It is difficult to be specific again and I have to resort to making some generalisations but my own experience having lived and worked in Britain all my life is that we as a nation don't really celebrate people who are successful, confident and assertive. I say this because of my experience on *The Apprentice*. The British press immediately used negative adjectives to describe this loud, confident woman with an assertive and passionate attitude, such as 'loud mouth', 'mouth of the South' and 'milk curdling monster'. Why was that? Why focus on the negatives? Why not focus on the fact that I achieved results and got things done? The British way is to draw attention away from the self rather than towards it. We love to support the underdog, and we don't like success when it's so in our faces. How do the British view someone who has a failed business? I think our attitude is that we wouldn't touch them with a bargepole. There's a stigma attached to someone who's failed; we don't focus on the fact that at least they had a go!

I feel that in Britain we are still too focused on people's class, their accent, their gender and their ethnic origin rather than their ability to succeed.

Drawing a comparison between the British and American way actually helped me to understand that in order to succeed I had to adapt and be flexible in my style to appeal to various people from different cultures and backgrounds. For a very long time I just didn't understand why me being loud, confident, passionate, driven and having a desire to win offended so many people in British business. I thought they'd jump at the chance to have someone like me. The fact is, however, that I wasn't really selling my ability and skills in a way that was attractive to British middle-class managers, who seemed to prefer a quieter, more determined approach to business. My approach was considered aggressive, which for a woman is not seen as a desirable quality.

Sometimes, I've despaired at the advice I've been given from managers to improve myself. Some have wanted me to be myself, others have told me to chill out more; some have told me to be more animated, others to be less animated; to be less passionate, to be more passionate; to ask more questions, to ask fewer questions; and the list of requests goes on and on. At the end of the day I have decided I have to be comfortable being who I want to be. I can't and shouldn't try to please everybody because that's an impossible task. I have to please myself first because if I'm happy with who I am then I can move forward and sell myself more effectively to others.

WHAT NOT TO SELL ABOUT YOURSELF

I've met enough people who seem to focus on what they haven't got rather than what they have got. It seems to me they actually enjoy being down as it gives them an excuse for people to feel sorry for them. I know somebody who always moans about the lack of money they have. They tell everyone the same thing: how they can't afford to do this, they can't afford to that, how hard life is. They've said it so many times that when their name comes up in conversation, the word 'moan' comes to my mind. That's the impression I take away of that person whenever I am in their company.

Selling yourself positively to other people is about making the right impression all the time, every time, and ensuring that only positive attributes are taken away in someone's mind. The only person who can do that is you! I believe that everybody has something unique to sell about themselves and can use that to create positive opportunities to get what they want from life. Every one of us has skills, life experience, opinions and ideas which, if presented to others in the right way, would lead to a successful experience.

The single most important point to remember when you interact with others is never ever to show people your insecurities; only show them your strengths. My experience has taught me that once you start sharing your insecurities with people, at some point they will use it against you to get one over on you. That may seem harsh, but unfortunately I've found it to be very true indeed. You should only open up your fears to those people you trust and who you know will help you rather than work against you.

Learning how to sell yourself positively takes time and experience. I want to share a really personal experience with you, which I believe demonstrates that insecurities are bigger in your own mind, and that others will never pick up on things about you unless you specifically point them out.

When I was 18 and at university, I developed a skin rash that affected my arms, thighs and back. I went to the doctors and specialists and tried all sorts of ointments, but all they did was calm the rash rather than get rid of it. It eventually started to affect the pigmentation of my skin and I developed white patches. For the next 16 years of my life, this pigmentation had a huge impact on my confidence, the way I saw myself and how I thought others saw me. I got down about not wearing the clothes I wanted, and it annoyed me that I had to moisturise my skin morning and night so that it didn't dry, crack and bleed. I couldn't shave my legs as they would get irritated; I had to have them waxed – what a chore!

In the summer months I used to stare at the perfect smooth skin my friends had. They wore lovely summer dresses that showed off their tanned legs. I, on the other hand, would wear long sleeves and trousers because I was so insecure about what others might say if they saw my skin pigmentation. For some bizarre reason, I used to tell people about my skin and point out the patches on my body so that they would understand why I was covered up. I didn't realise how obsessed I was about pointing out my imperfections. One day, my best friend turned round to me and said, 'Why are you always going on about your skin? You sound like a stuck record, for God's sake! No one really cares, you don't get asked about it so why the hell are you telling everyone? You've become known as "patchy Saira", and the funny thing is no one knew about your skin until you started doing your own PR on it!'

Well, as you can imagine, it was a bit of a shock to hear all that coming out of my best friend's mouth. It took me a few days to realise that, of course, she was absolutely right. Seventeen years on, I still have the pigmentation. The difference is that I don't go round telling people about it, and nobody has ever noticed it.

WHAT YOU SHOULD ALWAYS SELL ABOUT YOURSELF

Everybody has something they can sell positively to create better opportunities for themselves. The important point to remember is that if you want to be successful and a winner, you have to start acting and thinking like one. The fact is that when I was in *The Apprentice*, I didn't start every week saying, 'Oh no, I don't know if I'm going to win this.' I said, 'I'm going to win this even if it kills me.' Now, what kind of an impression do you think I gave people when I said the latter? It demonstrated drive, ambition, eagerness, energy, effort, desire and a passion to win. People who saw me every week saying that on television could see I was not an easy pushover. I am a great believer that if you want to succeed and impress, you only ever have one chance to make the right impression; it's very rare that you're given a second chance.

Let me tell you that there's nothing really very extraordinary about me. I'm not a great beauty; I'm not tall; I'm not a genius and I'm not everybody's cup of tea. I have my faults like everyone else. So how do I manage to get myself noticed? I focus on the things I know I'm good at and make sure that the person I meet leaves with a positive image of me. I take an interest in other people and always ask what they are doing; I get to know them better; I tell them about what I'm doing. I make positive gestures by remembering people's birthdays and sending thank you cards. I focus on what I can offer: my skills, my ideas and opinions and my life experience. Above all, I always make sure I try to turn a negative into a positive.

I remember at one interview I was asked if I could speak French. I said no, but continued to say that I was very willing to learn, and the fact that I could speak some Asian languages would put me in good stead. I managed to get the job over someone who spoke fluent French because I demonstrated a positive attitude.

Whenever I write an email, talk to someone on the phone, meet a new person or even a friend or family member, I always make the effort to be the best I can. I do it because I believe that if you make an effort for people they will make an effort back, and they will remember you for it. Focusing on the little things that people take for granted can really make you stand out from the crowd and the competition.

The important thing is never to feel that you are being a 'creep', a 'show-off' or an 'attention seeker' when you talk about yourself. For most people, talking to someone who is positive and confident about themselves is a lovely experience. Remember, it's better to leave a positive impression in someone's mind than a bland one. The whole trick is to find a balance between being forthright to promote yourself effectively and turning people off through excessive self-praise.

HOW CAN YOU SELL YOURSELF BETTER?

When selling yourself, the key is to be yourself and not to sell someone what you're not. That really will get you caught out, especially when you won't be able to deliver the expectations you've planted in others' minds. Be authentic and true to yourself. You can become better at selling yourself by focusing on three key areas:

- Skills
- First impressions
- Understanding others

Skills

In Chapter 2 I talked about having the right 'people skills'. You'll need to bring these into play when you sell yourself to others. Whether you are selling an idea or a skill or just want to leave a positive impression, knowing how to handle people is fundamental. Your questioning, listening and feedback skills will be crucial to ensure you get the person to deliver the response you are looking for. The two areas I want to focus on are the skills of planning and preparation and that of follow-up.

Planning and Preparation

Imagine you are about to paint an old window. The paint has cracked and is peeling away. What do you do?

- You quickly remove the peeling paint, rub the wood down with sandpaper and then apply the paint.

OR

- You protect the glass with masking tape, repair the wood if required, clean, prime and then paint.

I think the answer is obvious, but I bet there are many people who take the first approach and try to short-cut the process. The whole reason for prepping is to ensure your effort adds years to the life of the window. Furthermore, proper preparation will make it easier to apply the final coat and give you a professional finish.

The principles for painting a window can also be applied to real-life situations. Let's say you're going for an interview for a new job you really want. Well, the one thing that will get you noticed is your planning and preparation. I can't believe how many people out there don't prepare for job interviews. I've asked candidates simple questions like, 'So what is it about this company that attracted you to apply?' and the response has been a blank expression. Surely that's a very predictable interview question.

You can never plan or prepare too much. It's better to go over the top than do too little; at least you'll feel better for the effort. When I go for an interview I always prepare in the following way:

- Check the company's website for financial, personal and customer information.
- Check competitor sites to see what they are doing.
- Check details of the person who will be interviewing me.
- Seek out someone who works in a similar industry/department and get some tips on the industry and what's hot to talk about.
- Make sure I know the industry publication, get a copy and read it.
- Make sure I have my CV.
- Prepare questions to ask.
- Prepare answers for questions I might get asked.
- Research some interview tips if I haven't been to one for a long time.

■ Get a friend to ask me some questions so I can practise answering them.

■ Make sure I get a good night's sleep, my clothes are ready and I've checked on the time and place to meet.

■ Ensure that I know the route I will take to get there in plenty of time, i.e. train/bus times.

You can never short-cut the process. I tried to do that on *The Apprentice* and nearly lost out because of it. In episode 11, I was put through an interview, and one of Sir Alan's sidekicks asked me what I knew about Sir Alan's business. This really was a very basic question; the problem was that I just hadn't prepared for it at all. I only really knew about Amstrad, but he does a lot more than just make computers. I felt such an idiot, especially when the interviewer said, 'So you're applying for a job with an organisation which you don't really know a lot of detail about?' What could I say? I hate making excuses but to save my sorry self I said something pathetic like, 'Well, I just haven't had time to fully research him.' I could see he was not impressed at all! Luckily, I managed to perform excellently on all the other questions and the blip was overshadowed, but I never really forgave myself for such a stupid error.

Preparation and planning not only give you confidence but also show other people that you've made an effort, that you care and have high professional standards.

Follow-up

Following up is not the same as feedback. It means chasing up after you've completed a task, action or activity. I really encourage people to follow up because it stops them from fretting and thinking about what might happen rather than what is happening. I know that at some point you've experienced that horrible feeling at the end of an interview when you've been told, 'We'll get back to you soon.' Well, a week goes by and you're wondering, 'Did I get it? I bet I haven't, otherwise they'd have phoned by now? Should I ring and find out? No I can't, I might annoy them. It might show that I'm desperate. It might show that I'm too keen.' Personally, I always follow up with a phone call a few days afterwards to find out when I will know the result. At the end of the day, if I've made an effort then I expect people to make an effort back. Why should I be hanging around in distress? If they think being keen and showing eagerness is a negative characteristic, then it wouldn't be my type of company to work for. Even if you don't get a job after an interview, I still recommend that you follow up and ask for the reasons why, on this occasion, you were not a successful candidate.

I think this behaviour again helps you to stick in someone's mind. You just never know what may come of your follow-up actions. I mean, how many people do you think follow up after an unsuccessful interview and ask for feedback? The fact that you did puts your name in front of the interviewer again and in a positive light because it shows you care about your performance and have the confidence to follow up.

First Impressions

Research has shown that 60 per cent of successful managers are those who make a positive impression. The first impression is probably the single most important factor in determining your success. It takes only a few seconds but conveys an extraordinary amount of information about someone. Further impressions do count, but never as much as the first. First impressions convey your appearance, your attitude, your body language and your punctuality; a failure in one can lead to a negative first impression.

Appearance

Let's face it, we live in a world where the way we look matters as much as the way we think and act. In fact, some people decide who we are and what we are just by looking at us. Like it or not, that's the way it is, and I am a real advocate of making a good first impression through having a highly polished appearance. Your clothes, hair, nails and teeth all send their own signals, and they should always be those of a person with a mission to succeed.

Imagine you were at a party and met the following people. What would your impression of them be?

- Twenty-year-old female weighing about 18 stone, wearing ripped jeans and shapeless T-shirt, piercing on face, prominent make-up, mohican haircut.
- Twenty-year-old female, slim build, wearing a pretty, conservative dress, pearl earrings and necklace, light make-up, hair tied up in a smart ponytail.
- Twenty-year-old female, slim build, wearing a miniskirt, tight-fitting T-shirt and knee-high boots, strong make-up.

Now, let's imagine that the three turned up for an interview at your office to manage a sales team. What would your impression be of them? The point I'm trying to make is that your appearance should be adjusted to your environment, the occasion and people you have to impress.

I have my nose pierced, but I never wear my nose stud when I'm meeting people in a formal setting. I don't think it's about compromising who I am; I see it more as having a professional image and a social image. My nose stud is part of my social image; I don't need to wear it to work with my suit.

I don't think anyone needs to look like a supermodel in order to feel they have an acceptable image. Nor do I think people should lose their individuality or their freedom of expression. But I do think that being clean, smart and making the most of yourself will help leave a great first impression, and the effort and expense you invest in your appearance will always pay off.

I am always careful when I meet people from different cultures and religions. My experience has taught me that my appearance could unintentionally offend some people. As a young sales woman selling biscuits in the East End of London, serving a predominantly Muslim community, I made sure I dressed modestly so as not to embarrass my customers. I definitely did better than the previous female rep who served there. She refused to dress modestly and kept saying, 'Well, I just can't see why I have to. This is my country and they have to accept that I wear short skirts.' True as that might be, it wasn't helping her get what she wanted; and as I was more flexible and adaptable I didn't really see the big deal. If my customers wanted me to dress in a certain way and it helped me achieve my business goals, fine. I wasn't going to say no!

Passion

Passionate people tend to achieve their goals and ambitions. I believe that passion gives people direction, focus and drive. Imagine if you didn't have anything you were really passionate about, if all you did was work and live and you didn't enjoy anything outside of that? What would that say about you? I love to watch Chelsea Football Club, but more importantly I get mesmerised by the thousands of fans who yell at their team to win. For 90 minutes every Saturday, they show their passion. They get involved, they talk tactics, they read all the sports pages and they follow their team all over the country and even around the world.

My husband Steve is very controlled and measured, but as soon as you start talking about snowboarding he turns into a different person. His eyes light up, his voice gets stronger, he becomes animated and he can hold a conversation with a stranger about snowboarding for hours. He just goes into his own little world. The change in him is amazing to see. It makes me smile just to watch him, and I listen intently because his conviction is so strong that it's absorbing.

That's the beauty about getting passionate: it leaves a positive image in other people's minds and they remember you for having a passionate nature. No one sticks out in a crowd more than someone who is passionate. I am passionate about four things in my life: my family, my fitness, my work and social justice. These are the four things I can talk about all day and all night without tiring. These are my passions and some might even say my obsessions. These four things are what I wake up for every day and what make me want to strive in life. My passions are what I live for.

Attitude

You may be the world's best footballer, the best businessman or the most famous star, but if your attitude stinks and you haven't got the right frame of mind, then you just aren't going to get much further. Attitude is your approach to life, people, situations and experiences. If you think about the people who stick in your mind for positive reasons, they are probably the ones about whom you thought, 'I like your attitude.'

Again, having the right attitude can give you the edge when it comes to making a great first impression. It's common sense really. If you've got to impress someone, your attitude has to be exemplary. I've been described as having an assertive attitude, and let me tell you I don't mind that at all. There's a very clear distinction between rudeness and assertiveness, and sometimes people who are not used to dealing with assertive people mistake their behaviour as being rude. Being assertive means you say 'no' when you mean 'no' and 'yes' when you mean 'yes'. It means that you don't mind confrontation and you say it as it is to people's faces. I have always been like that. I don't see the point of talking behind people's backs. Some see my attitude as positive, while to others it is a threat.

One of the biggest failings I see in people is their lack of assertiveness. As a result, some people get walked all over and bullied, and never seem to get what they truly want from life. The best way of becoming assertive is to be really honest with yourself and say what you mean. It'll take time, but the more you start saying the things you feel, the more people will actually start to respect you for it.

Body Language

There are so many books out there on the subject of body language. This isn't surprising as between 60 and 80 per cent of our message is communicated through our body language, and only 7 to 10 per cent is attributable to the actual words we use. Your ability to read and understand another person's body language can mean the difference between making a great impression or a very bad one! It could help you in that job interview, that business meeting or on that date.

My only problem with analysing body language too much is that you could actually get hung up on it, and before you know it you've become paranoid about what your crossed legs say about you rather than being relaxed and yourself. I like to keep things simple. There are some basic things I always do to make sure my body language leaves people with the right impression.

Handshake: For me, the handshake is the most important thing. I've had to shake many hands in my life and I can tell you that some have left me feeling positively uplifted whilst others have made my whole body cringe! I like a good firm handshake; it tells me that the other person is confident, in control and honest. A weak or 'wet lettuce' handshake gives me the impression that the person lacks confidence, has low self-esteem and is not open. More importantly, they don't leave a strong impression in my mind. If there's one thing I recommend to everyone it is to adopt a good firm handshake. You will feel better in yourself for doing it.

Eye Contact: Have you ever been talking to someone in depth about a certain topic when the person you are talking to looks over your shoulder? How does that make you feel? What does that tell you about the other person? Making direct eye contact shows respect and interest in what the other person has to say, and it will also give people a feeling of comfort and genuine warmth in your company. It demonstrates to people that you are listening and focused on them.

Some people, however, may find it difficult to make eye contact because they are shy and lack self-esteem or confidence. In these situations it's important to be sensitive and encourage them to build up the eye contact gradually and when they are comfortable. I remember at university I fancied a guy, and whenever he looked at me I'd turn away because I was so embarrassed. I felt that if I made eye contact I'd give away the fact that I fancied the pants off him. He told me a few years later that because I never made eye contact with him he never bothered asking me out. He just thought I wasn't interested. I was gutted!

Posture: Droopy shoulders, a slouchy walk, crossed legs and arms are all no-nos for making a good impression. Your posture needs to be upright and open. This is more inviting and gives others the message that you are confident, open and honest. One of my bad habits is that I cross my arms when I'm feeling cold. I had to learn not to do that in interviews because it could give the impression that I was being defensive and closed to ideas. Sometimes when Steve and I have a heated discussion I automatically cross my arms, and he always picks up on it, saying, 'Look at your body language. You're being defensive.' He's normally right, which really gets on my nerves!

Facial Expressions: I use a lot of facial expressions, and it's good to be facially animated because people can engage in your passion and enthusiasm. Having limited facial expressions can leave the other person guessing about how you feel. The only facial expression that will always make sure you give a positive first impression is a smile. A smiling person is judged to be more pleasant, attractive, sincere, sociable and competent than a non-smiling person. A smile is a universal expression of happiness and recognised as such by all cultures; it also releases endorphins and makes us feel better. What would you rather be greeted by first thing in the morning: a bright, smiley face or a bland, expressionless face?

You should be careful of biting your lips or touching your face as it could give the impression that you are lying or hiding something.

Mirroring: If in doubt, the best thing to do when you are trying to impress someone is to mirror their movements and actions. If they are quietly spoken and use few hand gestures then mirror them; this will demonstrate that you are in tune and on the same wavelength as them. Mirroring is a technique all good salespeople are taught, and it helps them to build effective business relationships with their customers.

Body language is very important in selling yourself effectively to other people. I think I've mastered it over the years by observing myself in different situations. Some of our body language happens automatically as it's a behaviour ingrained in us from an early age. To change the behaviour from a negative to a positive you have to be aware of what you do, when you do it and what makes you do it. Once you can get to grips with that then you're on your way to making a change.

Being Punctual

Different cultures view the need to be punctual in different ways. I think we British are very serious about making a good impression by being on time for people. My mother is a real stickler. She can now proudly boast that in her 20 years of work at her local factory she never clocked in late.

I must admit that I am not a natural timekeeper, and there have been many occasions when I've turned up late for people and events. It annoys me when I do it because I feel disappointed that I've let other people down. I knew I'd got really bad when people started expecting me to be late. I didn't like having that reputation at all. It's really hard to shake off a reputation once you've been labelled in a certain way, but I have worked over the years to make an effort at being on time for family and friends.

Steve is a robot when it comes to being punctual. He comes from a very organised family indeed. When they say they'll be round at 6.30pm they are there at 6.30pm. I am always amazed.

It's not very nice waiting for unpunctual people, and I know I don't like it when people do it to me. In business, being late for work can really jeopardise your chance of a promotion. I was told by my manager once that the only thing letting me down in my performance was being consistently five minutes late for sales meetings. It demonstrated that I couldn't be bothered and I didn't have respect for my colleagues. All I needed to do was go to bed a little earlier the night before so that I didn't feel tired the next morning and to leave the house five minutes earlier to miss the traffic build-up. It's common sense really, but sometimes we just seem to lose sight of it and make it really hard for ourselves when it doesn't have to be like that at all.

Understanding Others

Selling yourself to other people is not just a one-way process. The other person has got to buy in to who you are and what you are selling. The best line I remember from my sales training is 'people buy people first'. You may have the best product or idea, but if the person you are selling it to doesn't connect with you, you won't have a chance. The key to being successful is to ensure you are adaptable and flexible to as many different people out there as possible, and that really does depend on the effort you are willing to make.

Acknowledge

In our society, we often overlook the importance of acknowledging other people. I think this leads to prejudice and barriers being created. The feeling that you are not being acknowledged is really horrible. When I was 16 I went to work in a factory with my mum during the summer holidays to make some pocket money. My mum worked so hard and I remember that the supervisor Ethel would come up to her and thank her for a good day's work. My mum never forgot Ethel. She used to come home telling us all how lovely and kind Ethel was, how she was the best supervisor there. Every Christmas, Ethel would get a bottle of her favourite Tweed perfume, and a bunch of flowers on her birthday from mum. Ethel was my first encounter with a good manager. She acknowledged everyone from worker to director with a smile, a 'please' and a 'thank you'.

I have always gone out of my way to chat to receptionists, cleaners, sandwich ladies, taxi drivers, shopkeepers, postmen, dustbin men and waiters because I think in our haste we forget to thank people and take their service for granted. When was the last time you had a really good chat to your waiter in your favourite restaurant? What do you know about their life? Believe me when I tell you that making an effort and acknowledging people can really help you get what you want, and people will really look out for you.

I worked in an office once where the car park spaces were taken on a first-come-first-served basis. Being five minutes late meant that I missed out on the best spaces. However, I didn't have to worry for long because Peggy, the receptionist, used to save me a space. She did this because she liked me – I always made time for her and asked about her family. I was the only person who had a regular chat with her every morning. There were 2,000 people who walked past her reception desk every morning and at least half of them didn't even know her name.

Share

My marriage to Steve is the best example I have of the importance of sharing and how it can help people from different cultures, religions and backgrounds come together and break down stereotypes and prejudices. My parents always expected me to marry an Asian Muslim man. I grew up in a culture where boyfriends and relationships were never discussed. My parents would choose my husband and that was the end of it. They didn't trust what they didn't know, and so marrying outside the faith and culture was the worst thing I could ever do to my parents. Respect in Asian culture is a huge issue, and girls are responsible for the respect of the whole family. So you can see that I had to deal with a lot of responsibility along with a great deal of guilt.

So can you imagine how I felt when I had to tell my mum about Steve? Steve is an Essex lad who doesn't care much for religion. The only thing he had in common with my parents was the fact that he loved a great curry! Telling my mum about my relationship with Steve was the hardest thing I have ever had to do in my life. I felt guilt and betrayal, and most of all I knew that I'd break her heart. Well, it was horrible. My mum was so upset. I remember her words: 'How could you do this to me? What will people say? How am I ever going to hold my head up high? You wouldn't do this if you loved me. If you go ahead with this I don't ever want to see you again.' My brothers and sister were great. They tried to explain that Steve was a nice guy and that there was nothing to worry about, but to no avail. She still would not accept it.

My mum's view of white English families was formed from what she saw at her factory, on television and in her street. She thought that the English weren't into long-lasting relationships and that when they got bored they just got a divorce and moved on to the next person. She felt that the English weren't interested in Asian culture, that if I married Steve I would stop being Asian and that I would get dumped by him when he got bored.

Steve could see the extreme pressure that I was under, thinking about the situation we were in all the time. I felt so torn between my family and the man that I wanted to be with, I just couldn't see a way out. I think it was the pure injustice of it all that made Steve decide to do something about it. We were both watching a film one Saturday when in the middle of it he burst out, 'Right, that's it, I've had enough. I'm going to sort your mum out!' and before I even had time to understand what he was doing he had called my mum on the telephone and told her that he was on his way to see her, there and then. Steve drove from London to

Long Eaton right away, without any planning, to talk to my mum.

He spent all day with her talking about his family, his values, how he was brought up, why he loved me, how he wanted to go and visit Kashmir and meet the rest of the family and how he'd been brought up to respect other people and be tolerant of differences. Well, after meeting Steve my mum was a different person. She phoned me up that night saying that she couldn't have asked for a better son-in-law. My mum broke away from all her cultural and religious traditions and even made herself the talk of the community to accept Steve. I know that people have talked behind her back and have said, 'How could she let her daughter marry a white guy who's not a Muslim?', and she's been very brave to take on all that crap. She's an amazing woman and I am very lucky to have a mother like her.

I have to give credit to Steve for making an effort to spend time with my mum and getting her to understand that not all white English families behave in a negative way. He shared his life and experiences with her and also demonstrated that he did share Asian values of family, respect and hard work. Our wedding day was a great occasion of East meets West. I wore a white dress, we had curry for our main course and even my mum got up and had a boogie. My wedding day was the best day of my life. I never thought I'd see the day when my mum would be so happy seeing me marry a non-Asian non-Muslim man. I am the only woman in the whole of my Kashmiri community in England to marry a non-Asian.

You may be asking, 'What has this got to do with selling yourself?' Well, in my opinion, the actions Steve took to win my mum around is a great example of the time, effort and passion required to get what you want. Steve could have taken the approach, 'Well, if your mum's not interested then we'll just do it without her,' or just decided it was too much hassle and perhaps called the whole thing off. But instead he took it upon himself to get my mum to see things from his point of view and was prepared to answer any of her objections. Selling yourself in this case was about Steve demonstrating to my mum that he was a genuine person, he was a family man and, above all, that he really loved me. Steve used his understanding and experience of the Asian culture and traditions and his knowledge about the Muslim religion to create common ground with my mum so that she felt respected and also respected him.

It is impossible to get what you want in life if you don't share yourself with other people. Sharing your thoughts, ideas and experiences with others allows them to trust and respect you and they are more likely to be receptive to what you have to say and help you achieve what you want. The value of sharing is ingrained in us as kids. How many times do you hear parents telling their kids to share? The reason parents encourage sharing is because it is seen as a very crucial behaviour to learn and to possess. As adults it's not always easy to share your ideas and emotions with others because we're all a little afraid of rejection or someone hurting our feelings, but the fact of the matter is that if you don't share, you will find it difficult to experience new opportunities in life and you will keep things bottled up inside, which leads to a whole host of emotional problems. Have you noticed that when couples are experiencing problems in their relationship they nearly always blame the other person for not 'opening up and sharing his/her feelings'? In work situations employees are frustrated by their boss because they don't know where they stand or what is expected of them because the boss hasn't shared his thinking with them. If you share you stop people second-guessing who and what you are and what you want to do. If you share with the right people, they may be able to help or offer you advice that may be useful to you.

The union between my family and Steve's has been an amazing experience. Sharing brings people together in amazing ways and helps build trust and integrity. Watching my mum share with Margaret (my mother-in-law) her secret recipe for making a good curry and watching Margaret tell my mum about her childhood memories of growing up in East London proved to me that it's the simple things that help you to achieve and get what you want in life.

Take an Interest

Next time you meet someone new and you get talking, be aware of how often the other person asks you a question about your interests, hobbies, experiences, etc. There were some people in *The Apprentice* who really stuck in my mind for always talking about themselves and not taking an interest in other people's lives. I remember once talking to a particular candidate for about 30 minutes about his family, his upbringing, his time at university, his hobbies and interests. I found out so much about him, being genuinely interested in him as a person, but do you know, he never once asked about me: 'So Saira, what about you? Tell me about your family and friends.' In that situation I felt that I had a huge competitive advantage over him; if he didn't take an interest in people then he wouldn't be very good at those tasks that involved people. I was right.

Taking an interest in other people's lives is another way to reinforce similarities. If people feel they have things in common with you then they will be more open to listening to you. If you think about the people you really warm to, they are probably the ones who take an interest in who you are and what you are doing. Those who take an interest leave an interest.

MY EXPERIENCE

The Apprentice Interview

Being picked from 6,000 wannabe apprentices and getting down to the last two demonstrates that I know how to sell myself effectively. The selection process for *The Apprentice* was a tough and competitive experience.

The First Stage

I received an email asking me to attend an interview at the St Giles Hotel in London at 6pm that Saturday. That was all I was asked to do; it didn't say anything else at all. I immediately thought, 'What am I going to wear? What will other people have on? How am I going to do my hair? Which questions shall I have ready? What are they going to ask me?'

The evening of the interview coincided with a friend's 40th birthday party, which gave me a real dilemma about how to present myself for this interview. The most important question I kept asking myself was, 'This interview is for a television programme. What do producers want to see in a person who will be appearing on television?' I asked Steve and he said, 'You should go dressed smartly but in something that shows you are confident, different and fun. Don't wear anything that's going to make you blend into the background.'

Apart from the 'what to wear' dilemma, the other two questions I felt I had to answer prior to the interview were, 'Why do I want to work for Sir Alan Sugar?' and 'Why do I feel I want to be on national television to do it?' I wrote down my responses to these questions and memorised them until I could repeat the answers confidently and directly.

I remember being really excited about the interview. When I walked into the hotel I saw about 200 people filling out forms, and it seemed a lot of them were wearing suits and carrying laptops. I walked in wearing a green and black summer dress, black strappy sandals and with my curly hair out in all its glory. I was definitely the least conservative dresser in the whole room and certainly did not blend into the background. I remember some girls giving me a snobby look. I smiled back. In my mind I kept saying to myself, 'Be happy, smile, be positive and be yourself.'

I was given a number and had to wait in line for someone to call me and take me in for the interview.

Whilst I was waiting my turn, I continued to look at the other people who'd attended. Everyone looked smart but they didn't look happy, nor did they look like they were enjoying themselves. It made me smile more.

Interview 1 – First Impression

I sat in front of Amy for less than five minutes before she said, 'Saira, I think you're great. I'm going to put you forward for the next round.' I couldn't believe it. She'd only asked me my name and why I thought I should be considered. A few months later, I asked Amy why she thought I'd be good in just five minutes. She said that she'd been sitting at the table interviewing people since 9am and I was the only person she'd met that day who'd walked in looking happy, excited and smiley. She said her task was to select people on her gut reaction and she had to ask herself, 'Would I get excited if I were to watch you on television for an hour?' I'd made the right first impression.

Interview 2 – Body Language

My second interview was with Charlotte. She really grilled me and asked loads of questions: 'Why do you want to do this?', 'Are you doing this just to get on television?', 'Why are you dissatisfied with your job now?', 'What are you looking to do in the future?', 'Tell me about your greatest achievements', 'What are your strengths?' Charlotte interviewed me for 20 minutes. At the end of all her questions, she paused, looked at me and said, 'I'd like you to go through to the next round, well done.' Again, I asked Charlotte why she chose to put me forward. She said that it was the way I answered all the questions: 'Your body language was really strong, you used gestures, you kept eye contact and you answered every question with energy and passion. I didn't see that in other people.'

Interview 3 – Sell Yourself

My final interview was with Dan. He was the main man (but I didn't know that at the time). Dan asked me one question, 'Why do you want to do this?' I looked him in the eye and said, 'Because I've got a story to tell.' He looked at me puzzled and asked, 'What do you mean?' I then spent the next 25 minutes selling myself, my background, my skills, my opinions and my business acumen. I was in my element talking about my experiences and what I hoped to achieve by going on the programme. I didn't leave any questions in Dan's mind about who I was and what I wanted. I remember Dan smiling at the end of the interview, and whilst I didn't want to jump to any conclusions, I felt deep inside that I'd done a good job.

I finished at 8pm and had been in interviews for two hours.

A week later I was sent an email saying, 'Congratulations! You have made it through to the next round. You are one of 40 people who have been short-listed for the final selection process.'

Interview 4 – Understanding Others

There were 10 of us seated around a table. We were told, 'This is the final stage of the selection process. Only one or possibly two of you will go through to the next round.' There were cameras in the room filming our every move and word. I had a good look at all the other candidates. First impressions were good: smart, polished and ready for business.

Our first task was to discuss as a group how we would turn an old people's home into a profitable business. 'We need a project manager,' demanded one loud man. I put my hand straight up. 'I'll do it,' I said. It takes a lot of nerve and confidence to put yourself forward in a group of strangers and start to lead. I wanted to demonstrate this side of me immediately as I felt it would certainly make me stick in people's minds.

Once the discussion started, I could tell the people who were being themselves and those who were not. Some were loud, some were quiet, some were moaning and some just gave the impression they couldn't really be bothered. Matthew and Adele were in my group, and when they started to talk and express themselves I thought they would be very interesting people to watch on television. They had confidence and didn't pussyfoot around; they told people how they felt and what should be done. Both had leadership qualities and were very strong people. I could see that not everyone liked them and some felt intimidated by them. I never showed anyone that I felt threatened by their presence, and focused on my own performance instead. I demonstrated the fact that I was a strong person too, but at the same time a personable one, and I didn't want to alienate anyone.

At the end of a long day, Matthew and Adele had stuck in my mind. I felt they were my closest competition. I got on with everyone at the interview; this was mainly because I'd made an effort, even though we were in direct competition. Some in my group, however, really did not gel. I found it interesting that in such an important round of interviews people couldn't put their prejudices aside to show their positive attributes. A week later I received a phone call telling me I had been selected as one of the 14 candidates to take part in *The Apprentice*. I was not told details of any other candidates. On the first day of filming I saw both

Adele and Matthew. We met up and all blurted out at the same time, 'I knew you'd get in!'

ACTION PLAN

See Chapter 1 for tips on getting the most out of these tasks. Use a separate piece of paper to write your answers to the questions.

Task 1: Face-to-face Meetings

To help you make a good impression all of the time, every time, you need to ask yourself the following questions, which will focus your mind on making sure that you are doing the things that matter, ensuring that you shine above and beyond your competition and ultimately get what you want.

Write down your answers to these questions. I have provided some examples of the things that you could write for each one.

- What kind of occasion is it?
- Who do I need to impress?
- What do I need to do to create a good first impression?
- What will I not do?
- What result do I want from selling myself today?

What kind of occasion is it?	Who do I need to impress?	What do I need to do to create a good first impression?	What will I not do?	What result do I want from selling myself today?
Social	Friends	Firm handshake	I will not talk negatively about myself	I want a new job
Formal	Family	Maintain eye contact	I will not shy away from a compliment	I want to get noticed by a specific person
Business	Colleagues	Concentrate on my appearance, shoes, clothes, hair, nails, scent	I will not be a wallflower	I want to meet new people and make new friends
Charity event	Boss	Make sure that I am dressed correctly for the occasion	I will not butt in while others are talking	I want to let people know that I've got the skills and experience they are looking for
Networking	New people	Have a clean and tidy car	I will not be shy in talking positively about myself	I want people to see me as confident
	Potential new boss	Smile and be positive	I will not hang around people I know all night	I want a promotion
	Foreign people who do not speak English as a first language	Be on time	I will not be lethargic	
		Do my research on the person I need to meet		
		Make the effort to meet new people		

Here is an example of what your table might look like:

What kind of occasion is it?

- Social

Who do I need to impress?

- Tom

What do I need to do to create a good first impression?

- Look my best, perhaps buy myself a new outfit and make sure that my hair and nails are done
- Smile and be positive
- Go and speak to him
- Make sure that I know what he likes and doesn't like

What will I not do?

- I will not talk negatively about myself
- I will not bitch about anyone
- I will not drink too much

What result do I want from selling myself today?

- I want him to ask me out for a date

Task 2: Selling Yourself over the Phone

If you need to sell yourself over the phone and make a great first impression, use this template to help you plan and prepare, to ensure you are registered above other callers.

Why am I calling?	Have I planned my call?	How will I sound?	Result I need from this phone call
To sell a product	Have I done my research?	Is my voice engaging?	I need a meeting
To arrange an interview	Do I know the names and titles of the people I need to talk to?	Do I sound cheerful and interesting?	I need to get the name of the relevant person
To complain	Have I got the necessary information at hand for reference?	Do I need to sound authoritative?	I need the person to remember my name
To provide information	How am I going to introduce myself?	Do I need to have a sense of urgency in my voice?	I need compensation
To introduce myself	How am I going to get past the secretary?	How can I stop myself sounding complacent?	I need information
To clarify	Have I prepared all my questions?	Do I sound friendly?	
	Have I prepared a way to overcome any objections?	How am I going to demonstrate I am listening?	
	How will I respond if I feel rushed on the phone?		
	Have I got my diary at hand?		

Task 3: Selling Yourself in Writing

Whether it's an email or a letter, you need to be able to sell yourself in writing. The template below will help you make sure you sell yourself effectively.

What is the purpose of the email/letter?	Have I got the basics right?	Writing style	What I need to remember	Result I need from this email/letter
Invite	Contact details	Formal	Have I stated a time by which I need a response?	I need acknowledgement
CV	Spelling of names and titles	Informal	Keep it short and to the point	I need an interview
Follow-up/ thank you	My own contact details	Business	Is there anything that could be misinterpreted in my writing?	I need feedback/ direction
Ask for a meeting	Date	Have I thought about how I could make my letter/email stand out?	Am I using quality paper?	I need information
To complain	Reference details	What font style is appropriate?		I need compensation
To provide a reference	Correct salutations	Do I need to attach my photo?		
To provide information	Have I attached/ enclosed the necessary information?			
To ask for information	Is my handwriting legible?			

SUMMARY

- Put yourself first and think about the qualities you have that make you stand out from others.
- Always sell the positives about yourself to other people.
- Be confident and proud of who you are – this will help you to sell yourself to others more effectively.
- Be aware of how you come across to others – focus on your first impressions.

4

Have High Standards

GOALS FOR THIS CHAPTER:

- ■ To set yourself clear guidelines and make the right choices.
- ■ To open yourself up to the right opportunities.
- ■ To be able to measure your success.

WHAT ARE STANDARDS?

What do we mean by having a standard? The *Oxford English Dictionary* defines standard as 'an established or accepted model, a principle of behaviour or morality, a criterion, a definite level of excellence, an authorised model for a unit of measurement'.

My dad used to say that one of the reasons the British managed to conquer half the world was because they were organised and worked to high standards. I didn't really know what he meant until I started to work in blue chip companies. There were performance standards, customer service standards, manufacturing standards, marketing standards. In fact, every department had standards that enabled people to measure how they were doing and what they should do to improve. Standards, however, don't apply just to work; they can be set in your personal life too. Having high work and personal standards is another way to shine above your competitors and make a positive impression on people. Setting high standards tells other people that you aim high in life and you choose to live by a certain set of rules that are important to you.

We all unconsciously have standards and never question why we do things in certain ways. However, we can start to make improvements only when we become conscious about what we do. Imagine I asked you now, 'Can I have a look at your bedroom?' Some of you might say, 'Yeah, no problem, go ahead,' whereas others might reply, 'Um, yes, fine, but please mind the mess. I haven't had time to do the bed yet and my clothes are all over the place.'

The way we go about our ordinary day-to-day activities gives clues to others about our organisational skills and how we choose to live. Personally, I think it's really hard to maintain high standards all the time. We are human beings, after all, and not robots. Having said that, there's always a need to project the better side of yourself when it really counts.

PUTTING HIGH STANDARDS TO WORK

Standards in Institutions

In Britain we have some amazing institutions that uphold the highest of standards and, as a result, are way ahead of their competition when it comes to quality of service and respect for its people and brand. For me, the BBC is a great example of where its standards have kept it as the leading force in the media industry. It always amazes me how many of us trust and depend on the BBC to bring us up-to-date quality news reports, educational programmes and great family entertainment. So how does the BBC get it right consistently? Well, it's simple: it's because at the heart of everything the BBC does it works to a set of high standards which guide people on how they should behave as an employee and how they should treat their work and other people they work with. The standards have been revised as and when necessary to keep them relevant and up to date. People all over the world respect the BBC and a lot of that is down to the high standards the BBC upholds.

The BBC's editorial standards are as follows (for a full breakdown visit www.bbc.co.uk/guidelines/editor ialguidelines):

'The BBC is committed to delivering the highest editorial and ethical standards in the provision of its content and services on all platforms both in the UK and around the world.'

Importantly the high standards relate to the following:

- Truth and accuracy
- Impartiality and diversity of opinion
- Editorial integrity and independence
- Serving the public interest
- Fairness
- Privacy
- Harm and offence
- Children
- Transparency
- Accountability

These standards inform the public of what to expect from the BBC and when we feel that they have not performed to the standards that have been set out, we as the public have clear measures on which to base our feedback, criticisms and complaints.

Standards in Our Own Lives

I have come to the conclusion that anything business can implement to improve employees' performance and efficiency can be used in our personal lives to achieve the same objective. It makes absolute sense. For example, the BBC standard of being fair and impartial, open-minded and respectful is certainly one that most of us could incorporate into our lives to become better people. To take another example, I find it amazing how many parents don't seem to care about the standards in their children's schools. If you don't know what their standards are, how do you know the school is serving your child better than any other school in the area? If, for example, you know that your child's school has a standard that states 'There will be no more than 30 pupils in each classroom', would that satisfy what you are looking for when choosing a school? What if another school stated 'There will be no more than 20 pupils in each classroom'? Then which school would you prefer to send your child to?

The point I am making is that some people live their life by having high standards and some just don't give it a thought. Having high standards demonstrates to other people that you are an individual who is in control of the choices that you make in your life and that you pay attention to how you want to be perceived by others. I have experienced the way in which personal standards affect the way others treat, respond and interact with you. For example, have you noticed how the assistants in expensive shops are always well presented and immaculate looking? What does that tell you about those shops' standards? How does it make you feel when served by an assistant who is well-groomed and wearing smart clothes?

If you live in a house that is well looked after and things are put away neatly in their place, what impression are you giving to the people that come round and visit? It tells them that you are well organised, you care about your personal space, you are a good time manager and that you want visitors to respect your space. Other people will judge you on your standards and it is therefore crucial that you think about them and make sure that you are not giving the wrong impression. The best example that I can give you to highlight this point is that of the former Labour Party leader Michael Foot. Despite his many achievements in life it's actually his unconventional appearance that people think of when his name is mentioned. I think that's a real shame.

Life is hard at the best of times, but my theory is don't make it harder for yourself by taking a 'can't be bothered' attitude. If you choose to be obese the fact is that you are actually telling others 'I don't exercise, I don't care about my health, I have little self control and self respect'. Cruel as it may sound, obese people are limiting their chances of gaining other people's respect. I can tell you from my experience that if I had been overweight it would have limited the number of opportunities that came my way for television programmes I could be involved in and also I would never have caught Steve's eye. Some of you may say that this is superficial and people should look under the surface and not judge people by the way that they look. I would agree to a certain extent, but I would also point out that you need to be the best that you can and show that to others. Why be fat when you can be thin? Why limit your opportunities when you could open yourself to so much more? Why let your weight decide what you can and can't do when you could be open to everything if you weren't overweight?

Being honest with yourself about your standards and what they tell others is a great starting point in making a positive change. It's no good saying, 'Well, I don't care if people think I have no self control because I am fat,' because that is not going to get you anywhere. The approach to take is, 'I am really pissed off that people aren't giving me a chance because of my weight. I'm going to do something about it and prove I have self control. If all I have to do is lose weight then I'll do it.'

I think that our standards are greatly inherited from our parents and the environments in which we develop. If you grow up listening to classical music it's very likely that your taste in music will be influenced by that experience. If you've been brought up by parents who have high standards in cleaning, chances are that you will probably be very house proud too. But, as I have said throughout this book, you can always improve the way you are in order to enjoy the quality of your life and get more of what you want and enjoy being successful.

My mother-in-law, Margaret Hyde, is an amazing woman. She has inspired me to have another look at some of the ways I do things. Her whole life is based on having high standards. Here are just some that I have observed:

- She never goes to anybody's house empty-handed. She's always got something to give to her host when she visits them in their home.

- She never forgets birthdays and anniversaries.
- She makes an effort every day by putting on her make-up and wearing a nice outfit.
- Every night she sets the table – with a tablecloth, napkins, candles and flowers – and cooks a fresh meal.
- She reads the *Guardian* every day and keeps herself updated on current affairs.
- She is never late.
- She gathers the whole family together every summer for a golf and petanque weekend, and cooks all the desserts for the event.
- She is the best hostess I have ever met; her standards of welcoming people to her home and creating a magical experience are very hard to beat. Even if you are just passing by and pop in to see her she will make you a cup of tea served in her best china with a piece of homemade cake. Nothing is ever too much trouble.

At 67, Margaret has more energy than some 30-year-olds I know. My standards in music and literature have improved because of her, and I've also taken pride in making sure I'm a good hostess when people come to my house. I would rarely have gone to the effort of making the table look so nice if my mates were coming round, but since seeing Margaret's table-setting standards I have followed suit. The greatest pleasure I get from the effort is comments like, 'Saira, the table looks gorgeous – thanks for making it so special.' People remember good high standards.

SETTING GOALS

One of the most important things I've learnt in business is how to set goals to improve myself and my performance. I remember my first training day when the trainer spent a full day on the topic of setting goals. At the time I thought, 'Here we go again, another bit of business jargon I'm never going to use.' Well, I had to eat my words because my whole business career has been about setting goals and putting together an action plan for achieving them. Setting goals helps you achieve the standards by which you are looking to live your life. You may be thinking, 'I can't believe that just by writing down a goal I'm actually going to change something about my life.' My response is: TRY IT!

Your View of Yourself

How many times have you actually sat down and really thought about the person you want to be and the life you'd like to lead? Have you ever written down how you see yourself? If not, try it. Which words would you use? Let me tell you there is nothing more powerful than seeing what you think about yourself on a piece of paper. If you are not happy about what you see written down you are more likely to do something to change it.

How do I know this? Well, there was a period in my life when I was feeling really down and depressed. My father had died; I was in a job I didn't like; and my relationship with Steve, whom I'd known for a year, was very much on and off. I just felt like I'd had enough of everything and everybody. Sometimes when you feel so low it's hard to find a solution to your misery, but I've always been one to help myself out of a rut. Keeping all the worry and tension in my head made me feel confused and I just couldn't see a way out at all. I started to write down all the things I didn't like about myself and what I had to do to make myself feel better:

- I am too dependent on Steve for my social life. I need to make more effort to go out with my own friends.
- I feel out of shape and I need to exercise more, at least three times a week.
- I am not happy at work and I want to do something more with my life.

I remember that as soon as I wrote my problems down I felt my mind was so much clearer, like a burden had been lifted from my shoulders. Seeing what I had to do to make improvements made me feel a lot better because I could then see that the steps I had to take were very achievable.

SET YOUR OWN GOALS TO HELP YOU:

- Get out of a rut.
- Take control of your life.
- Prioritise the important things in your life.
- Feel successful, regardless of what that means to other people.

Successful people use goals to aim high, set high standards and achieve the success they are looking for. One of the most interesting books I have read is Clive Woodward's *Winning*. In it he describes how he set about changing the face of English rugby, with England then going on to win the Rugby World Cup. Throughout his book, he shares the goals and high standards he set for his team, and demonstrates that without having these in place it would have been very difficult to motivate and inspire them to succeed.

Set Yourself a Personal Goal

If you are going to set goals properly, there is a process that has to be followed: a goal cannot be achieved unless it is specific, measurable, action-orientated, realistic and timed.

In the business world, the way to remember these criteria for setting goals is to use the acronym SMART. This stands for:

- **Specific** – Define precisely the objective or outcome you want.
- **Measurable** – Define objectively how you will know when you've attained it.
- **Action-orientated** – Use action verbs to describe the steps required.
- **Realistic** – Confirm your belief that the goal is indeed possible.
- **Timed** – Set a deadline for reaching your goal.

Always check that the goals you set yourself are SMART. In this way you will ensure they are likely to be achieved. Here's how I made my goals SMART.

Goal: I need to make more effort to go out with my own friends.

Specific: At the moment the way I've written that goal is not going to encourage me to do anything about it, apart from keep reminding myself that I need to make an effort to go out with my friends. To make it more specific and get myself to understand exactly what it is I want to do, I really need to say: **I need to go out with Alison, Josephine and Beth.** This is specific. It tells me exactly which friends I need to go out with.

Measurable: The next questions I need to ask myself are: 'How will I know I'm actually achieving my goal?' 'How do I measure if I'm successful?' 'If I go out with my friends once a week, will that satisfy me or is that too much?' You need to think about setting yourself a realistic target. The measure I chose was, to **go out with my friends at least twice a month.** This was enough for me to feel I was making a concerted effort.

Action-orientated: Achieving goals means you will carry out some form of action to make it happen. It's no good having goals if you are not going to do anything about them. The action I have put into my goal is that **I am going to go out.**

Realistic: Realistic goals are crucial because if they are not being achieved you will feel demotivated and stressed. Setting realistic goals means you can do what you actually want to do. So, for example, I need to make sure that going out with my friends twice a month is a realistic goal. If I have booked myself up every day and have only one day in a month to see my friends then I can't achieve my goal of trying to see them twice a month.

Timed: Setting a time limit for your goal means you are giving yourself a deadline to complete your activity. This will help you see how you are progressing. So in order to make my goal smart, I need to expand it: **I need to go out with Alison, Josephine and Beth twice a month for the next 12 months.**

So my original goal which stated, **I need to make more effort to go out with my own friends** is now SMART and reads, **I need to go out with Alison, Josephine and Beth twice a month for the next 12 months.**

SMARTening up My Other Goals

This is what my other goals look like in their SMART format:

- **Non-SMART goal:** I feel out of shape and I need to exercise more, at least three times a week.
- **SMART goal:** I will go to the gym three times a week and do 30 minutes of cardiovascular exercise for the next 12 months.

- **Non-SMART goal:** I want to do something more with my life.
- **SMART goal:** I will take up tennis lessons and play in the local club league in the next 12 months.

Try not to set yourself more than three goals at any time. Learn to achieve a little at a time, otherwise you will feel there's too much to do and it will demotivate you.

Reviewing Your Progress

I am one of those people who love to be busy. Although I can multitask well, there are times when I'm very busy but not actually achieving significant results. This is because I've lost sight of the real goals. One way of making sure I stay on track with my performance is to ask myself the following three review questions regularly:

- What is expected of me?
- How am I doing?
- What can I do to improve?

By answering each of the above, you can ensure you stay focused on your goals and stick with them until they are achieved. It's critical that you review yourself because if there are things you are not achieving, you may have to revise some of your action points. To show how this review process works I have put together an example.

Long-term Goal: To increase the amount of physical activity in my life every week and incorporate this into my lifestyle. I want to be exercising three times a week every week by the end of this year.

Week 1: Targets
- Walk the kids to school every day.
- Use the stairs rather than the lifts when shopping.
- Walk around the block at 7pm every evening with my friend.
- Buy a book on basic health to improve my understanding of how the body works, and read one chapter every week.

Week 2: Targets
- Read another chapter of the book.
- Buy an exercise video and use it for 15 minutes every morning as my friend can't make the 7pm walk.
- Concentrate my exercise on my bum, tum and arms – these are my problem areas.

■ Get my husband to join me to help me with motivation and support – and we can challenge each other.

Week 3: Review My Performance

1. What is expected of me? I need to increase my physical activity to every evening.

2. How am I doing?

Target	Achieved	If Not, Why Not?
Walk the kids to school every day	Yes	
Use the stairs rather than the lifts when shopping	Yes	
Walk around the block at 7pm every evening with my friend	No	Friend not reliable, calls up at last minute and says she can't make it
Buy a book on basic health to improve my understanding of how the body works, and read one chapter every week	Yes	

3. What can I do to improve?
   ■ Set myself more challenging targets.
   ■ Push myself to do the activity even when I don't feel like it.

■ Find another friend to walk around the block with me as current friend is not reliable and I feel disappointed when she lets me down.

SKILLS CHECKLIST

Setting goals is important but achieving them is the key to success. I always find it easy to start things in my life, but more difficult to complete them. The main reasons for this are:

■ I get distracted.
■ I come across barriers.
■ I lose momentum.
■ I lose focus on the purpose.
■ I find it hard to motivate myself all the time.

The best example of this is when I decide to start a detox programme. I begin really well: I do all my reading up; I get all the ingredients; I write down what I am going to eat every day; and I make sure I am in the right frame of mind. Day one goes really well and I feel proud for sticking with the detox programme. Day two is okay. Day three is tricky because I get called out to meet a friend for a coffee. I tell myself I'm only going to have a herbal tea and no cakes. I see my friend munching away on a lovely chocolate cake and the coffee smells lovely. I lose willpower and order the same. I've failed and it's only day three. Does all that sound familiar to you?

There are other goals I *have* managed to complete, so I've asked myself why it is that I can achieve some and not others. Well, I've worked it out: the essence is that the goal will be achieved only if you really want it, and if you possess the skills you need to make it come alive.

The following ingredients are essential for anyone who wants to achieve their goals in life:

- Passion
- Planning
- Persistence
- Patience

Passion

I have mentioned the importance of passion before, but you have to be passionate about setting your goals and achieving the standards by which you want to live. If you're setting goals just because you think you should, then I can tell you that you won't succeed. Passion is what keeps your dreams and goals alive and gives you the desire to keep going even when it's tempting to give up.

Planning

Achieving goals requires planning. In some cases, you might need the help of other people, so you'll have to make sure they can get involved and plan for their time. Sitting down and giving yourself time to plan your goals and formulate an action plan is crucial. You just can't do it any other way.

When I started to write this book my editor, Julia, asked me for a plan of each chapter to show her what I was going to write about. I thought, 'Why do I need to waste all this time on a plan when I could just get on with writing the chapters?' I found putting the plan together really hard work, tedious and time-consuming. After a week I managed to finish it and still couldn't see the point. Julia assured me that I wouldn't have been able to write the book without it. She was absolutely right: my planning gave me a clear focus, direction and path to follow. My thought process was so much clearer because I knew exactly what I had to write about. It's the same with writing down goals: once you have planned and written out each step you need to follow to achieve them you will give yourself a much higher chance of success.

Persistence

Goals and standards don't happen overnight. In fact, success doesn't happen overnight, even though the media sometimes lead us to think otherwise. Some of you might say, 'Well Saira, you achieved overnight success with *The Apprentice*.' My response would be 'Rubbish!' I am 35 years old. I've had years of people telling me, 'You can't do this and that, you're no good at selling, you'll never make it in the business world.' I've won some battles and I've lost some, but my persistence has kept me going. My ability to pick myself up, dust myself down and start again has been a key factor. I don't let others pull me down. I have never given up on learning and being the best salesperson I could be. It takes time, and all the hard work has paid off because I wanted it to and because I believed in myself and my ability. Persistence pays off.

Patience

I am one of the world's most impatient people. If results don't come quickly, I get demotivated and bored and I'm on to my next goal. I am impulsive by nature, saying the first thing that comes into my head, and if I want something, I want it now. I hate waiting for things to happen. My impatience has got me into some serious hot water, and as a result I have had to programme myself to be more patient.

The best thing I have ever done to improve my patience is to coach people in sales. Coaching requires patience because the people you are training take time to improve. You see a gradual change in people's performance; it doesn't happen in a matter of hours. It used to annoy me that some people would take so long to get the hang of selling, but being patient with people and encouraging them bit by bit was rewarding when they finally managed to get their first order all by themselves. There's no better feeling than when the whole plan just comes together.

Goals can take a long time to be achieved. Provided that you tell yourself from the start that things will take time, you should be mentally prepared. There's very clear reason why you should learn to walk before you run: each stage has to be completed before moving on to the next or you jeopardise your chances of success.

MY PERSONAL STANDARDS

As I have matured and taken lessons from my life experiences, I have become very clear about my own standards: the standards by which I want to live and for which I would like others to respect me. Living by your own standards is not easy. I'm certainly not saying that I live up to mine all the time. But the important thing is that I do have a very clear notion about what I represent, and I try very hard to live up to these standards.

Health

My health is very important to me and I make sure I exercise at least three times a week. My friends and family know me for keeping fit, and I have a go at them if I know they are not looking after their health. I have made career choices based on the single fact that a job will give me the opportunity to exercise after work.

I make a concerted effort to cook well and eat well. Every morning I make sure I have a good breakfast, which is the most important meal of the day. I go to the dentist and I have my necessary checkups at the doctors. I do all I can to make sure I have high standards when it comes to my health.

Some people may think I'm really moralistic and straight because I don't do drugs, get drunk every Saturday night and just let myself go. Well, that's fine. I am proud to have high standards, and if people think that's boring, I let them think it because I know who I am and what's important to me. I'm not bothered about fitting in or belonging to a group. I follow what's right for me.

Relationship

My relationship with Steve is the most important thing in my life. Like any married couple we've had our ups and downs and faced some very challenging times. We have set high standards for our relationship and we both work very hard to make sure we involve each other in our lives. Although we are both strong-minded and independent, our shared focus on high standards keeps us together. We are both into sport; we are both close to our families; and we make sure we make time for each other.

During and directly after *The Apprentice*, I didn't see Steve very much at all. I could see how if I continued being away so much we'd end up drifting apart and start leading two separate lives. So we did something about it. Every Thursday, Steve and I go on our 'date night'. It's our night when we give each other our full attention and create that feeling of going out with each other again. It's brilliant; we both really look forward to it. We both dress up for the occasion like we used to when we were first dating. I think a lot of us drop our standards when we get together with our partners; we get lazy and start to take people for granted. It's something I'm aware of and I do my very best not to fall into that trap.

Family and Friends

I've become closer to my family as I've got older. Without their support and love it would have been impossible for me to reach this platform in my life. I speak to my mother and mother-in-law every other day; we have regular family get-togethers; and we make time to see each other. Again, there are politics and fallings-out in every family, but you help each other out because you're family.

My real friends have been with me through thick and thin. Their love and support have been incredible. *The Apprentice* really brought me closer to my friends and family because I found they were always there for me no matter what, cheering me on every week and making me feel positive and happy even when I felt I hadn't performed so well. The really successful people I've met are those with high family values. I've met some very lonely people who have the money, house, clothes and cars, but not much else. No money in the world can buy you the love of your family and friends, and it's for that reason I have high standards when it concerns them.

Personal Appearance and Space

My self-respect and personal hygiene standards are reflected through my appearance. I look good for myself first. The way I represent myself to others in a physical way is very important to me. When people meet me I want them to think, 'She's smart, polished, confident and respectable.' I want people to notice and acknowledge me, and I have found that having high standards in my personal appearance does help me get more of what I want out of life. I never leave the house in the morning without making up my bed; I make sure I have fresh flowers in the house every week; and I don't let the dishes sit in the sink waiting to be cleaned. I make sure my car is clean and smells nice and that my desk at work is organised. I do this for my own self-respect and pleasure. It makes me feel good and confident about myself.

Reliability

To be an excellent salesperson, I need to be reliable for my customers. If I'm not then I'm jeopardising my own credibility and my own standards. Reliability can make or break a business deal or relationship, and it's a good foundation on which to build trust. Being reliable means that I do what I say and see that it happens that way. It's amazing how many people will bullshit their way to get business, and then when it comes to delivering they just aren't reliable. Once you get a reputation for being unreliable, it's very hard to shake it off.

MY GOALS

Running the Marathon

Five years ago I could barely run for more than 10 minutes. In April 2004, I ran 26 miles in 4 hours and 33 minutes and completed the London Marathon. It was one of the most amazing experiences of my life, but I have to tell you that the training and commitment tested me physically and mentally. Steve had run the London Marathon in 2002. It was one of those things he'd always wanted to do before the age of 40. I remember he was absolutely thrilled when he'd achieved this goal. Having watched Steve do it I felt that I'd like to give it a go too. It would demonstrate to me and to others how serious I was about my own fitness. Steve decided to do it with me and act as my training buddy.

When I saw the marathon training plan I was a little horrified at the amount of running I had to do. The furthest I'd ever run was about 10 miles, and I wasn't the fastest of runners. Steve and I sat down and started to write a training plan and set personal goals. We had given ourselves four months to train for the marathon, and this is what my typical week looked like during that period:

- Monday: Run for 45 minutes at a steady pace
- Tuesday: No running, weights only
- Wednesday: Do a hard hill run for 45 minutes
- Thursday: Rest day
- Friday: Do speed training for 45 minutes
- Saturday: Rest
- Sunday: Do a one-and-a-half-hour run at a good fast pace

All this training took place after a hard day's work. If that wasn't difficult enough, I had to control my diet and force two litres of water down me. The first week went very well, but then it got harder and harder and harder. I was training in the winter months and there were times when I just wanted to lie in rather than run 15 miles in the pouring rain, but Steve would push me out of bed and get me started. I began to get bored of the same old routes as I'd know how far I still had to run when I got to certain points. There were many times when my legs would hurt so much that I'd cry halfway through the run, but I never stopped. This went on for four months. My whole purpose in life was to plan and prepare for the London Marathon. As I achieved my goals one by one, I felt an enormous sense of achievement. When I ran my first ever 20 miles I felt so proud; it was the furthest I'd ever run in my life. But the pain of training was unforgettable. I soon realised that running was more of a mental exercise than a physical one. When I felt tired and ready to give up, my brain would kick into action and I would talk myself through the reasons for not stopping. The biggest challenge I found was to keep interested in running.

I decided I would try and run the marathon in under four hours; this would be a realistic yet stretching target. So on the big day I felt prepared and ready to go. I felt confident that I had done all the necessary planning and training. It was a huge bonus that Steve was running with me because having a buddy in training really helped me to carry on running at times when if I had been on my own I may have given up. I did run very well, but I found the last five miles so hard, I can't begin to tell you the complete mental exhaustion I felt; my legs were tired and I just wanted the whole thing to end.

My pace did drop towards the end so it was Steve's persistent encouragement that made me determined to finish what I had started. I was 33 minutes over my target. I was really disappointed with myself because I didn't hit my target of four hours and felt I could have done better, and in hindsight I wish I'd tried harder to keep going rather than giving up mentally towards the end. I could see that Steve was disappointed with me a little bit too. I knew I had slowed him down. If he'd been running by himself he could have finished that marathon in 3 hours and 15 minutes. I felt bad about letting him down but at the same time I felt really happy that at least I could say that I had completed the London Marathon. Now that I have experience, I am determined to run a marathon again and beat my time of 4 hours and 33 minutes.

The whole marathon process made me realise that despite all the odds I can do anything I put my mind to, as long as I am passionate, can persevere, plan and have patience. I proved to myself that I can achieve my goals but that it is not always an easy ride, and that there are times when even the most self-starting people need help from time to time to keep them focused, inspired and motivated. I think the most important thing that I realised about myself is that even if I achieve my goals, that's not always enough; I have to prove to myself that I have done the best that I can and hit my target, otherwise I won't get a sense of real satisfaction.

ACTION PLAN

See Chapter 1 for tips on getting the most out of these tasks. Use a separate piece of paper to write your answers to the questions.

Task 1 – Assess What You are Doing Now

Use the template below to gain an understanding of
what your current standards are and explore why they
are like that. There may be some things you are happy
doing, but ask yourself, 'Could I do them better?' The
following list will get you started but you can add other
areas you feel are important to you.

Standard	What do I do now?	Why?
Health		
Appearance		
Personal conduct		
Time-keeping		
Self-development		
Conduct with others		
Personal living space		
Inside of car		
Desk at work		
Garden		
Outside the home		

Task 2 – Assess Where You Want to Be

Next, write down what you would like your standards to be – here are some examples. Prioritise the standards that are most important to you.

Standard	What do I want the standard to be?	Why?
Health	I want to improve my health and make it a focus and priority in my life	Because having good health will open up more opportunities for me
Punctuality	I want to be on time every time for my friends and family	If I improve my time for others it will show that I care about other people and make an effort
Inside of Car	I want to make sure the inside of my car is clean	Anyone getting inside my car will see I take pride in my belongings and they will treat it with respect

Task 3 – Assess How and When You are Going to Improve Your Standards

Write down the SMART goals you need to set yourself to achieve these standards (see page 155). My biggest tip is not to set yourself too many goals. Set yourself three and once you have achieved this then move on to the next ones. The achievements of your goals should not be temporary; they should be permanent and become a way of life. Use the following template to write down your goals, targets and action plans. Here is an example.

SMART Goal: *To improve my physical health in the next 12 months and make it an essential part of my life thereafter*

Targets	Actions
Take a multivitamin tablet once a day every day	1. Buy relevant multivitamin by taking doctor's advice
	2. Make a note on the fridge door to remind myself to take one
Join the local gym and go three times a week	1. Get a personal trainer to discuss the right exercises for me
	2. Make time in my diary and let nothing get in the way
Work specifically on certain parts of my body	1. Record my ability now and record how I am doing every time I use the gym to monitor my improvements
	2. Record the physical change in my body and how it makes me feel
Train with a partner	1. To keep me challenged and motivated get a friend to come along and work out with me
	2. Get competitive to get better results

Task 4: Assess How You are Doing

You must take time to review your progress with the goals you have set yourself. Be honest with yourself and write down how you feel and what's stopping you from moving forward. Make yourself find new ways of doing things. Don't be scared to ask people to help and support you. I have found that people are often willing to help others achieve goals that are really important to them. Use the template below to review yourself.

What is expected of me?	How am I doing?	What can I do to improve?	The four Ps
Insert SMART Goal here	How are you doing against the targets you have set yourself?	What can you do do to improve your performance and stay focused on your goal?	Which of the four Ps do I need to focus on to help me achieve my targets (see page 162)?

SUMMARY

■ Identify your standards – make them a trademark which sends out a specific message to others about the way you do things and how you should be treated.

■ Set SMART goals to achieve what you want and give you control over how and when you carry out tasks and activities.

■ Understand that goals are achievements and that they take time to achieve. Remember, Passion, Planning, Persistence and Patience will help you through the hard times.

■ You can always improve your standards – observe people whom you respect and see if there are things they do that you could adopt to help you improve the way you currently do things.

5
P.U.S.H.
for a Vision

GOALS FOR THIS CHAPTER:

■ To have a goal in your life.

■ To find a focus and direction for your energy and efforts.

■ To be able to measure your success.

Where do you see yourself in five, ten, fifteen years' time? Do you see yourself happily married with kids? Do you see yourself living abroad? Do you see yourself running your own business? Or do you see yourself in the same position and nothing really changing?

Having a vision has given me direction, focus and the ability to aim high. My visions have helped me to better myself. I never once thought I'd spend my life in the council house where I was brought up. I wanted to move away and do well for myself; I had absolutely no doubt about that. Having a vision of what you want from your life can help you plan and prepare for it; it gives you a path to follow; it keeps you focused on what's important to you; and above all, it makes you think big.

I compare a vision to a dream. A dream is our ideal – what we really want for ourselves – but for some of us it disappears when we open our eyes. It doesn't have to be that way. The fact that you have a dream is an excellent starting point. It is a sign that you have a vision for yourself.

A vision is where you want to be in life. It's when you think, 'If I can achieve that, it'll be amazing, it'll really make me happy.' At the start, a vision could be something that seems unlikely. For example, if some-body had told me five years ago I'd be writing a book to help people recognise and realise their potential, I might have said, 'Yeah right, I'll believe that when it happens,' but I wouldn't have considered it impossible. I'd have been able to visualise it happening and realise it was a goal to work towards that could happen over time, if I wanted it to.

EVERYONE SHOULD HAVE A VISION

Having a vision isn't a tool to be used just by business people. It's a tool that everyone can use, whether you are a single mother, a teenager, a retired couple or a person with an illness. Having the ability to visualise can help you get out of a rut and strive for a better and more rewarding life that you imagine for yourself. It gives you something to live for and think about; and it can make your mind focus on the positive rather than thinking, 'I'm never going to be able to achieve that, it's impossible.'

Sportspeople

Sportspeople have a vision in their mind and then set about making it come true. Dame Kelly Holmes is a fantastic example of this. Her vision to become an Olympic champion came true when she won the gold medal for the 800 and 1,500 metres in Athens in 2004. It took 20 years to make her dream come true. When she received an honorary doctorate in Sports Science from Leeds University in 2005, she said, 'You can have dreams and goals and you can achieve them. Life is not easy. You will always come across barriers but these barriers can be overcome... Give yourself a chance of achieving your dreams.'

What's inspirational about Dame Kelly is the fact that she doesn't come from a privileged background or a celebrity family. She's an ordinary woman who has achieved her vision by applying herself to what she believes in – herself and her ability. Simple. She didn't get her rewards for free; she worked very hard for them.

There is a big link between successful people and sport. The discipline of aiming high and having a single focus to achieve that aim can be used in all walks of life by all sorts of people. Sportspeople have to build their success in gradual steps. They don't just go to the gym, have a workout for a couple of hours and are then ready for the Olympics. Their regime is relentless: they have to watch and measure what they eat, beware of illness and injury, train every day, even on those days when they really don't want to. They have to compete at all levels and sometimes deal mentally with the fact that they didn't win, and work out what they have to do to improve. They have to have the self-belief, strength of character and mental ability to keep going and overcoming all the negatives. It's not easy, but what keeps them going is that vision of winning and being the best in their sport.

True success does not happen overnight. It comes after years of hard work, commitment and desire to make it happen.

People with an Illness

Do you know someone with a serious illness? When you visit them, what do you say? Do you find it hard to talk about the future with them because you think they might not have a long future? Well, my personal advice is that all people should be encouraged to think ahead and focus on positive thoughts. Just because someone is ill doesn't mean they can't be happy or have a dream or vision about what they'd like to do when they get better. My mum told me that moments before my father died in hospital, she was talking to him about what they were going to do and where he'd like to go once he felt better. My mum said my dad was in real pain but she could see in his eyes that talking about getting better lifted his spirits and calmed his anxiety.

My mum went into a very depressive state after my dad's death. There was a stage when my brothers and sister felt that we might lose our mum because she was so heartbroken. She'd lost the only man she'd ever loved, and it felt like she'd given up on everything and everyone when he passed away. My mum kept saying things like, 'I just can't see how my life is ever going to be the same. I'm going to be so lonely. How am I going to survive and what will my life be like without my husband?' We helped Mum through it by painting a vision that showed her that her life would be different but that she would still be happy, and that she would be able to do the things she wanted to even though dad wasn't around. As a family, we spent a very long time helping her out of her rut. We stuck together, never giving up on her and constantly providing her with a vision of what she had to look forward to, such as grandchildren and spending time with them. My brother told her he would move in with her so that she wouldn't be on her own. We helped her see that she could afford to spend six months in Kashmir with her family and six months in England with us, and so she had the freedom to do what she wanted, when she wanted. Helping her to visualise all these possibilities really helped my mum become herself again. It was a hard and painful process, and we took her development step by step. We helped her over the painful times like birthdays, Christmas and anniversaries. Again, we focused her mind on all the good memories we had of dad and what he'd want Mum to do. I am happy to say that she is once again the mum I know and love. I know that when she saw me on *The Apprentice* she was overjoyed that I'd done so well. She kept saying, 'Your dad would be so proud,' and I know she could picture his reaction in her mind. In cases where people can't see the light at the end of the tunnel it's important to try and help them do so, because when they can you know they are on the road to recovery.

Businesspeople

One of my most memorable experiences of the power of having a vision happened when I was working for United Biscuits. The sales force had been taken over by two new, dynamic directors who had been brought in from a competitor to improve the sales performance. Some of the older salespeople felt really threatened by this as they feared redundancy and any change.

Edward Brown, the new Financial Director, had a tricky situation to deal with. He wanted to make changes but he didn't want to scare or demotivate anyone. His keynote speech to the 200-strong sales force was therefore crucial in getting the message right first time. It was a speech I was never going to forget.

Edward created a vision of what he wanted the sales force to achieve. His vision was 'flawless execution', and he set out what this looked like and the benefits it would have on the sales force. He created a vision where people would be rewarded on their merits, results and performance; he created a vision of a highly organised and powerful sales team that could respond quickly in a fast-moving industry; a vision of the most aggressive yet customer-focused sales force in the country. He created a vision of how we would celebrate if we were to hit our first-year targets. It was such a strong vision that I felt I could touch it there and then.

It was one of the best motivational speeches I have ever heard in business. Interestingly enough, under Edward Brown I was promoted four times in two years and achieved the best results of my career.

Famous Visionaries

Some of the most incredible people have made their visions a reality against all odds. People like Martin Luther King, Mahatma Gandhi and Nelson Mandela had visions that must have seemed impossible to people around them. Through their focus and relentless drive, however, they achieved the impossible.

Martin Luther King's 'I have a dream' speech must be one of the most famous visions ever articulated. It was so vivid and real that people could see what had to be done to make it come true. He talked about boys and girls from different backgrounds holding hands and being united, and being treated equally regardless of their race. He talked about people of different races sitting together at the same table and getting on. King had this vision in the 1960s when black people could not walk on the same side of the street as white people in the southern states of America. The speech inspired and motivated a change to make the vision a reality.

HOW TO SET A VISION FOR YOURSELF

To be able to visualise properly, you need to be in tune with your body, mind and soul. You should be aware of your needs and wants, and be able to think deeply and connect with yourself. This is really important as it will make it easier for you to recognise and realise what you want from yourself and how you see yourself in the future.

Step 1: Prepare to Relax

Find a quiet spot where you can relax and think without getting distracted. You need to be in a frame of mind to really think about your life now and in the future.

Step 2: Ask Yourself Questions about All Aspects of Your Life

Close your eyes and think about where you see yourself in five years from now. Ask yourself questions about all aspects of your life, for example:

- Purpose of life
- Relationship
- Spirituality
- Hobbies and interests
- Possessions

- Finances
- Home/location
- Health and fitness
- Career/job
- Family
- Friends
- Self-development

Be honest with yourself and aim high for what you really want. If you want to work for the United Nations then visualise it. Don't think, 'Oh, that'll never happen. I can't see that for myself!' Think big for yourself because then you will achieve big. Nothing is impossible, but if you're not even prepared to think it and write it down in the first place, it will always remain inside you where it can't be acted upon.

Do you think I would have made it to the final of *The Apprentice* if I didn't aim high? I went into that competition with the vision to win and that's it: no ifs and buts, just to win! I threw myself at that vision. I did everything I could to make that vision happen. Although I didn't come first, I got what I was looking for: the chance to work for myself, make my own decisions and help others recognise and realise their own potential.

Step 3: Capture Your Thoughts and Write them Down

Now write down on a piece of paper the thoughts that came into your head when you asked yourself questions about all the aspects of your life.

Step 4: Prioritise

Go through all the different aspects of your life and come up with a list of prioritised areas. If an area is low on the priority list it doesn't mean that it gets forgotten and you don't deal with it. Instead you give it attention later rather than sooner.

Step 5: Take Action

Now take the first item on your list and develop a plan around it. If it is financial, talk to a financial adviser. If it is a career issue, talk to a trusted friend or someone who understands your career goals. In any case, talk it through with a coach, mentor or expert in the area. Search out books, educational programmes and other useful resources, and study them. Whatever you do, make sure you start doing. There are too many people in this world who think and plan and say, but very few doers. Becoming a doer will make your vision come alive.

Review and Revise

Review your plan regularly and make sure your vision and plan are what you want them to be. You might want to add to or amend part of your plan. At least once a year, review your entire plan and adjust your priorities. This should enable you to see how you are moving towards living the life you want and being the person you want to be. You might find it useful to ask your partner or someone very close to you for some feedback. How well do they think you've done? Feedback often makes me look at things in a different way and gives me ideas for becoming better at what I'm trying to do.

Vision Contract

I have already mentioned the benefits of writing down your thoughts. I recommend you go a step further and write down the visions you have for all the different aspects of your life, creating your very own 'vision contract'. I like the word 'contract' because it's authoritative and serious. When you make or sign a contract, you do so after much thought and deliberation, and you proceed only if you are 100 per cent sure that you agree with what the contract says. That's how I think you should view your vision contract. It's no good writing down your vision and then forgetting all about it in

six months' time. What's the point of that? You're not being true to yourself and you are demonstrating to yourself that you weren't that serious about achieving your goals in the first place. What you're really saying is, 'I can't be bothered to make an effort. It's easier just to accept whatever life throws at me.' If you break your vision contract, you have only yourself to blame.

I have put together the following vision contract as an example:

- I will be a good person and be happy.
- Happiness to me means being close to my partner, family and friends, and spending quality time with them regularly.
- I will have a comfortable home which is open to my family and friends.
- My home will be a place where I find peace and solace. I will live in a clean and tidy environment.
- I will raise my children to respect people regardless of their age, sex, religion or ethnic background.
- I will help my children with their education and sport.
- I will help my children appreciate that there are people less fortunate than them and ensure they understand the importance of charity.
- I want to be financially independent and will run

my own business. I will give 10 per cent of the profits to Save the Children, which will help to educate girls around the world.

■ I will be involved with local community affairs and will one day stand as a local councillor.

■ I will be fit and healthy and careful about what I drink and eat.

■ I will be a spiritual person and will be in tune with new ideas and practices.

■ I will be IT literate.

■ I will retire at 55.

Signed _____

Dated _____

How to Keep Your Vision Alive

I have shared my vision with my husband, and I talk about where I want to be in my life with my family and friends. I think by doing that you keep the vision alive and at the front of your mind. Here are my tips for making sure your vision is real and not on a piece of paper in the cupboard:

■ Print it out and share it with those people who are close to you: your husband, wife and

children. Sharing your vision with other people will help them to help you achieve it, but remember that you should only share it with people that are supportive and positive about you.

- Keep it in a visible place in your home so that you don't lose sight of it.
- Amend and review it as your life changes and some of your visions are realised.

MY VISION

My vision for my life has been the same for as long as I can remember: I've always wanted to get married to the man of my choice, have kids, run my own business, have a comfortable house, be healthy and happy and have my family and friends around me. It may not sound like that's aiming very high, but coming from a humble background, financing that vision and making it a reality is a massive achievement. The decisions I make in life are based on that vision. I have taken up some opportunities that have brought me closer to my vision, and I have turned some down that I felt took me away from what I want from my life in the long term.

Steve and I have a shared vision of how we would like our life to be. We have both decided that we don't want to be working into our sixties so we want to retire in our early fifties. We are planning to have children when we are a bit older, so we want to make sure we are around for them when they are growing up. This vision has made both Steve and me take some very serious decisions. We've decided that we want to work from home and for ourselves. Based on the desire to make this vision come true, Steve quit his highly paid corporate job and set up as an internet consultant. He works from home, takes holidays when it suits him and makes his own decisions. It also means that when we have kids, he will be around at home to be an active dad, which is very important to him. He couldn't visualise himself having children and then seeing them only when they were in bed.

This vision of having a family also spurred us into buying a small chalet in the French Alps. We could have put the money into a bigger house in England but we decided to stay living in our small house and buy the chalet. This means we have a place for the winter to do snowboarding and also somewhere to take our kids in the future for summer and winter holidays. We thought the chalet was a better long-term investment and fitted in with what we want from life.

So you see, if you have visions of yourself in the future, then you can plan and make decisions to make that vision into a reality.

I have also found that visualising a future event or activity helps me to relax and become emotionally prepared. The best example of this is when I knew I was going to be in the final of *The Apprentice*. I was aware that I had a 50–50 chance, but to make sure I was totally prepared, I sat down and imagined how that final boardroom event would take place. I visualised where I would be sitting, what I would be wearing, what Sir Alan might say and what my reaction would be if I won or lost. I visualised my reaction over and over again. I knew that, whatever the outcome, I would want to be seen to take the news in a mature way and restrain myself from the predictable outburst. Whatever happened, I didn't want my reaction to alienate the other finalist, Tim, in any way.

So I visualised myself being a mature loser and mature winner. What would my face look like? Would I smile, cry, put my hands over my mouth in disbelief? I visualised this for days and days. In the end I decided I would react with dignity, which meant I would smile politely at whichever decision was given to me and then immediately hug Tim. On the night of the final, that's exactly what I did. I wasn't nervous and I wasn't shocked because in my mind I had prepared for whichever decision was thrown at me.

ACTION PLAN

Task 1: Think about Your Life

Take a few days to think about all aspects of your life. Go through each one and write down where you want to be in the next five, ten, fifteen years. It is difficult for some people to see so far ahead, so plan for the timescale that feels comfortable for you.

My tip is always to **AIM HIGH** and to write down your aims. Never think, 'Oh that'll never happen' – if you want it to it will, as long as you set yourself goals, focus on them and start doing something about them.

Write your vision contract (see page 190) and keep it in a place for you to see every day. For example, use it as a screen saver, put it on your laptop, keep it in your diary or put it in a frame on your desk. Don't be afraid to share it with other people and don't be embarrassed about it. This is what you want from your life and you should be proud of it.

Task 2: Visualise for Confidence

Write down an event or situation you are involved in that is very important to you and makes you feel nervous.

Write down what it is about the event that makes you nervous. Is it the number of people? Is it the fact that you have to make a speech?

Close your eyes and picture what you think it's going to be like. Make it real. Visualise the following to help you:

- How you feel – awkward, excited, sad, happy, shy, nervous
- What you are wearing
- What the room looks like
- What the people around you are doing
- How you are interacting with other people
- What the atmosphere feels like
- What you are going to say and do
- The reaction to your actions from people around you
- What you are going to eat and drink
- How you want the event or situation to develop
- Before the event or situation, try and find out as much as you can about it. This will help make you feel you are not entering a completely cold environment and that you are better prepared.

Visualise in this way whenever you feel anxious, nervous or lacking in confidence. It will help you to relax and feel more in control.

SUMMARY

■ Always aim high in life – you'll achieve more in this way.

■ Make time for yourself to review and reflect where you are going in life.

■ Write down your vision contract and keep it visible. Only share it with people you trust and who care for you.

■ Visualise events, situations and people – this will help you feel more prepared and confident when you are nervous or anxious.

6

P.U.S.H.
for Your Values

GOALS FOR THIS CHAPTER:

■ To have a clear understanding of what's important to you.

■ To be able to make decisions about your life more easily.

■ To set your own rules for what happiness means for you.

WHAT ARE VALUES?

We all spend a lifetime accumulating our own unique set of values. Our values are shaped by our experiences, from our upbringing and culture to our education and working life. These values influence our choices about what we should prioritise in life. I am always amazed by celebrities who have everything money can buy yet seem to suffer from loneliness, failed relationships and addictions to drink and drugs. I think the reason so many of them lose the plot is because they have forgotten what's truly important to them – what makes them happy and fulfilled. It seems to me that many of our values sit dormant in our minds and are not really acted upon until something drastic happens.

My Father's Death

Have you lost a parent, child, friend or close family member? Well, if you have then you will know that nothing can ever prepare you for the death of a loved one. In 1998, I was like any other ordinary 28-year-old living in England. I had a good job, a good salary, nice friends and was enjoying my life. I was independent and didn't have to be responsible for anyone except myself. Life was great.

In July 1998 my parents decided to visit Kashmir. They had never been back there together in 30 years, so this was a really special trip for them. I remember my dad giving me a hug and telling me to look after myself: 'You're the oldest. You have to set the example and look after your brothers and sister.' I didn't realise that this would be the last time I would see him alive.

At 3am on 28 December, my brother Masood picked up the ringing phone and came running into my room, absolutely panic-stricken. 'Dad's dead. He's had a heart attack!' is all he said. I just felt numb. I remember thinking, 'It can't be true, they've got the wrong family. Someone has phoned us by mistake. It's someone else's father that's died.' Within an hour of that news reaching England, our family and friends were round at our house. They booked our tickets to Pakistan to attend my father's funeral. I remember sitting on the plane and looking over at my younger brothers and sister. Masood was 27, Sajdah was 25 and Tariq was 23. They had all lost their father at such a young age, and for the first time in my life I felt very, very responsible for them.

After a 16-hour journey we arrived at the village in the foothills of the Himalayas. We found our mum and saw our father wrapped in a shroud. I'd never seen a dead body before and I remember thinking how peaceful he looked. I leaned over to kiss his face. He was so cold that it made me cry because my dad never liked the cold. Watching as the rock of your family is buried is an experience I can't put into words. All I can say is that from that moment I became a different Saira Khan.

My dad was the leader of our family. He gave us direction; he made the decisions; he was the one we all wanted to please; he was the one whose approval really mattered; he was the motivator and the one who set the standards. He provided the roof over our heads and paid the bills, and was the focus for family and friends visiting us. He was everything. I lost everything meaningful in my life in one day. You never know what you've got until you lose it. I took my parents for granted; I took my life for granted, and I didn't really think about what was driving me.

My dad's death made me look at life and people in a completely different way. It made me question what my purpose was in life; why, despite my good job and income, I felt empty inside and unfulfilled; why I felt I hadn't really achieved a lot in life. For the first time I realised what it meant when people say 'life is too short'.

I am the person I am today because my father's death made me question what I was doing and what was important to me. My family became the centre of my life. I became very aware of my actions, behaviours and thoughts and I made decisions in my life with them in mind. I wanted a high enough salary to be able to give some money to my mum and help her out. My self-development became important. I didn't just want a good job and salary; I wanted to work where I felt I was contributing to people's development as well. I put a plan together of all the things I'd been meaning to do but never managed to get off my arse and make happen. I spent six weekends on an exercise-to-music course and qualified as an aerobics teacher. I went travelling around the world by myself for a year. I started to support a few charities, and made sure I spent more time with my family and got more involved in their lives.

Part of everything I do is driven by the fact that I want my father to be proud of me. Even though he's not here, I have a huge responsibility to respect his name. I am his representative and I know he would want me to focus on the values he held in high esteem. His values were family, honesty, love, respect, generosity of heart, health and success. These are my values too. Everything I do centres around them. So, for example, if I'm asked to appear on a certain television programme I don't just say, 'Oh yes, I'll do it for the money.' I say to myself, 'If I do this, how will it affect my family? Will this programme allow me to be honest and is it going to be respectable? If I do it will it contribute to my success or will it jeopardise it?' When I did *The Apprentice* I went through the same process. I decided to go ahead because it was a respectable show about business and it was a BBC production. I talked to my family about it and they encouraged me to take part.

My values give me the backbone to go out and do what I feel is important to me. I don't do it to please others.

IDENTIFY WHAT'S IMPORTANT TO YOU

If someone asked you to strip bare for a thousand pounds, would you do it? Whether you would or not, your values would influence your decision. Now that's not to say you're right or wrong, good or bad. The point is that at certain stages in your life, some values are more important than others. For example, I know that before my father died, my family was important to me but I didn't really make the effort I do now. In my early 20s, whilst I was trying to establish myself financially, I used to take a job based on the salary because the pursuit of money was the key driver in my life. Now that I'm better established financially I can make more informed value judgements and decisions. I would now choose a job based first on whether it would allow me to share my skills and talents in a positive way. The money consideration is still there, but it's not such a priority as before. I have taken voluntary jobs to give me experience, skills and networking opportunities. I would never have even considered that in my early 20s.

When you think about your values, consider what's important to you now and in the long term. In that way you'll be able to focus on how your priorities will change as you change with your life experiences. If you are a parent, you will know that taking responsibility for a child alters your whole outlook on life; things you never even noticed before suddenly become very important. I noticed this change in my sister. She used to swear like a trooper, eat what she wanted when she wanted, and spend lots of money on lovely clothes and shoes for herself. She was a real career girl, working and living in all parts of the world. Now that she's had a baby, well there's no swearing in the house, television programmes are censored, every bit of food she buys is checked for additives and her topic of conversation revolves around the best nurseries in her local area. She's decided she wants to spend more time with her child and so has made the decision to work for herself and from home.

Your values should be based on what's really important to you rather than what you think other people would like your values to be. Be honest with yourself. Your values can't be wrong or right because they are what suit your individual life. If you value money and that's what drives you, that's fine, don't just say it's not important because your friends think that charity is more important than money. Everybody is different and it's our life experience and our upbringing that shape what is integral to us and what we will prioritise in life. A good example to demonstrate this is the debate on eating organic produce. I would like to guess that most of us care about the state of the environment and if the price was right we would all love to buy organic food. However, if you have the money and time to buy it, it will be an important part of your values to eat well, but if you live on a budget, have a large family and live in an area where organic food is not easily accessible then it won't be high on your list of priorities, because what will be important to you is buying food that suits your budget. In both these scenarios neither is right or wrong.

I think it is important to add here that there are *some* values that are wrong and in my list I would include the following:

- Dishonesty
- Cruelty
- Prejudice
- Disrespect

Look through the list opposite and tick the values that are most important to you but choose three that are critical. To help you do this use the following ranking procedure to help you choose the three most important values to you.

RANKING INDEX

1 Not very important

2 Somewhat important

3 Important and would like to have in my life

4 Very important; critical to include in my choices to success

Feel free to add your own to the list:

☐	Adventure	☐	Keeping promises
☐	Ambition	☐	Learning
☐	Being faithful	☐	Love
☐	Creativity	☐	Money
☐	Challenge	☐	Passion
☐	Family	☐	People
☐	Freedom	☐	Power
☐	Friendship	☐	Recognition
☐	Fun	☐	Religion
☐	Health	☐	Respect
☐	Honesty	☐	Security
☐	Humour	☐	Success
☐	Independence	☐	Travel
☐	Integrity	☐	Trust

PEOPLE WITH STRONG VALUES

When it comes to living by values, my role models are people like Mohammad Ali, Sir Bob Geldof and Sir Alan Sugar.

Since becoming a black Muslim, Mohammad Ali has lived by his religious values. He has drawn his confidence and strength from his beliefs. He went to prison rather than serving in Vietnam because he didn't feel it was right to go into someone else's country and get involved with their political situation. He has talked about his religious beliefs proudly and used them to justify his progression and success. His values have also helped other people around him, who did not share the same values, to understand his point of view and know what – and what not – to expect from him.

Sir Bob Geldof's values have caught the imagination of the whole world. Once the lead singer of the famous Boomtown Rats, he is now an expert on African poverty, influencing politicians from across the globe. His passion for his values can be seen every time he talks on the subject. He has persuaded and influenced people to give their time and effort to the cause, and people have been moved to action because they share his values.

Sir Alan Sugar may not spring to mind as a man who has values, but having worked for him, I can say he holds his values in very high esteem. Honesty, trust, family and charity are the key values that were apparent to me. These values drive his business and personal decisions, making him a remarkable businessman.

MY VALUES

I have used my values to help me live the life I want with the person I want. Have you been in that situation when you've been going out with someone for ages and you ask yourself, 'Is this the right person for me?' On what do you base your decision? Is it the fact that they are good in bed, financially independent or have a good sense of humour? Is it based on whether they share the same religious values? Well, believe it or not, I had a mental tick-list of the things I was looking for in my future husband, and if all the important ticks (values) were not met then I wasn't going to commit. I asked myself:

- Is he family focused? Does he want a family one day?
- Is he fit and healthy? Does he go to the gym regularly?
- Is he financially independent or does he have loads of debt?

- Does he have drive, ambition and want to be successful?
- Does he have a sense of humour? Can he make me laugh?
- Is he the kind of person who will mix in well with my family?

It may sound like there was no love or emotion involved in my courtship with Steve. That's not the case, but in my mind there was a set of iron values that had to be met if I were to marry this man. I wasn't going to make the biggest decision of my life based on whether he was cute, good in bed and had nice nails. I am happy to say that my values served me well.

DEALING WITH UNPLEASANT PEOPLE AND SITUATIONS

There are people in life who will support and guide you and want the best for you, and there are people who will be happy to see you upset and in pain, and will rejoice in your misery. This is life's reality. The only way you can identify the good from the bad is to make judgements based on your own values.

I have met some wonderful people but, unfortunately, I've also met some very nasty ones. My values of honesty, truth and respect have helped me identify the people I need to keep close to and those I need to shut out of my life. If you have strong values and live by them, it's really easy to spot those who don't have values and who will do anything for selfish reasons at anyone's expense. I have met so many people in business who will lie and cheat to get their next promotion, and who will not care about their colleagues or even give them credit. Business is competitive and ruthless at times, but it doesn't mean you have to be a nasty person to operate in it.

I once worked for a very large telephone directory company as an advertising rep. Although I enjoyed the job, the managers were probably one of the worst groups of cliquey people I have ever come across. Their management style was just short of intimidation – patronising and bullying. They did this because it kept their positions safe and cosy, and they protected each other from any complaints or allegations against them.

The staff turnover for the company was very high, which reflected the way people were treated. The managers tried to explain this by saying that staff turnover is always high within sales departments. That may well be true, but when your company's turnover is 60 per cent and the industry average is 30 per cent, that tells a different story.

I stayed in that job for six months. Even though I couldn't afford it and didn't have another job to go to, I decided to leave because I just couldn't work for people who were lying, cheating and intimidating. At my exit interview I told the truth about why I was leaving, but deep down I knew my comments would never reach the relevant person. The internal politics of some companies I have worked for have shocked me, but they have also motivated me to work for myself. I just knew that if I wanted to live by my own values and standards I'd have to create a situation which would allow me to do that.

Living by your values is not always easy. Growth can be painful and uneven. You will make mistakes and fall short of your own high expectations. Despite the best of intentions, you will backslide into bad habits. Living by your values does not guarantee a trouble-free life. Living and leading with your values requires the maturity to accept that there will be temporary setbacks. Sometimes we have to operate within a system that is unethical, unprofessional and unfair, and our personal circumstances sometimes make it impossible for us to just get up and leave. The most important advice I would give anyone in this situation is never to compromise your values – you will never forgive yourself.

ACTION PLAN

Task 1: Find Your Values

List your most important values and write down why they are important to you. How do they make you feel? Use the grid on page 207 to help you.

Task 2: Identify Short-term and Long-term Decisions

Write down five situations that will require you to make a decision in the near future. For each one, ask yourself if the decision will affect your life in the short term or in the long term.

Task 3: Make Your Decisions

Write down the decisions you are going to make for the above situations based on your values. Remember, never compromise your values.

SUMMARY

- Identify the values that are important to you and live your life by them – this will give you a sense of purpose.
- Make difficult decisions based on your values – this will be beneficial to you in the long term.
- Use your values to deal with difficult people and

situations. This may be hard, but you will feel better within yourself, knowing you did what was right for you.

■ Never compromise your values. Never.

7

P.U.S.H.
for Success

GOALS FOR THIS CHAPTER:

■ To be able to define what success means to you.

■ To have the tools to learn how to measure your success.

■ To learn what success means to other people.

WHAT IS SUCCESS?

To me, success is achieving my vision and living by my values. It's that simple. I want to be a successful person: happily married with kids, living in a nice home, spending time with my family and friends and working in a capacity where I can help people recognise and realise their potential. I want to be able to spend time doing the things I enjoy like keeping fit, travelling, writing and presenting. I want to be always learning something new, and ensuring that every year I have at least one achievement I can be really proud of. If I can achieve all that, then I will feel successful.

For me it's not about living in the biggest house with all mod cons and driving the flashiest car. It's not about being seen in celebrity circles and wearing the latest clothes. It's not about having the most money or the perfect body. It's about leaving a positive, lasting impression in people's minds when they meet me. I want people to say, 'She's a nice girl that Saira Khan. She's hard but she's fair.' That's the biggest compliment anyone could ever pay me. When people say that to me it makes me feel my dad would have been proud of me, and that the sacrifices he made to come to this country and give me a chance in life were not in vain.

HOW CAN YOU MEASURE SUCCESS?

Since the age of 18 I have kept a small diary which I fill out religiously at the same time every year: on 1 January. In that diary I write down my significant achievements during the past year. This is what my diary looks like so far:

1988   Passed my driving test and went to university in Brighton.

1989   Became financially independent – got a week-end job and worked as a foreign-language teacher during summer holidays.

1990   Just being a student.

1991   Graduated with BA (Hons) – went to Nottingham University to study for a Masters Degree.

1992   Graduated and moved to Brighton. Got my first proper job working as a town planner.

1993   Living by myself in Brighton and working, making new friends.

1994   Bought my first property in Brighton and acquired a tenant.

1995   Started new town planner's job working for firm of solicitors. Learnt Italian at night school.

1996   New career change, working in sales for Burtons Biscuits in Bracknell.

1997   Moved to London to work for United Biscuits, my second job in sales.

1998   Father died. Was promoted at work after six months in role. Gained fitness instructors' qualification.

1999   Two promotions this year, now Area Sales Manager for Central London with eight direct reports.

2000   Met Steve. Went snowboarding for the first time and bought my second property in London. Became an aunt.

2001   Headhunted to work for a field marketing company, responsible for a national sales team.

2002   Travelled in Southeast Asia on my own. Visited 14 countries and learnt to scuba dive and trek in rainforests. Did a bungee jump. Saw rare animals and the wonders of the world.

2003   Came back and moved in with Steve. Got engaged to Steve. Started new career in advertising. Left after six months and joined an IT company selling online recruitment.

2004   Applied to *The Apprentice*. Got married. Steve and I bought a chalet in Chamonix.

2005   Book deal with Random House. Became a columnist for the *Daily Mirror*. Made television pilot for BBC. Panellist on Radio Five Live. Set up www.wsibusinessinternetsolutions.com with Steve – our own business, which helps people to simplify the internet.

When I look at my life like this I get a great deal of personal satisfaction. I feel that every year I have moved forward with my goals and have pushed myself to achieve my vision.

Success to me is also the impression other people have of me. I know I am being successful when people around me use the words I want them to use to describe me. Success to me is leaving a positive image in another person's mind. It's when people talk highly of me when I'm not there. The words I want others to use about me are:

- Energetic
- Positive
- Enthusiastic
- Competitive
- Has a can-do attitude
- Gets things done
- Makes an effort
- Strong
- Open-minded
- Caring
- Generous
- Focused
- Excellent salesperson
- Proactive

- Fit
- Healthy
- Stands up for herself
- Inspirational
- Motivational
- Committed
- Passionate
- Informed
- Insightful
- Resourceful

WHAT STOPS PEOPLE ACHIEVING THEIR GOALS?

I have met some extraordinary people: some who have a particular talent or skill; some who are intellectual; some who are naturally very beautiful; and some who seem to have all the beauty, brains and luck in the world. But what strikes me is that despite all these gifts, they seem to plod through life, not making the most of what they have and what they could be. They spout excuses, blame everything around them for their misery and rut, and act like victims of circumstance.

The key things that separate me from these kinds of people are my overpowering self-belief and confidence. I have decided that I want to be a winner, a success and the best I can, and that nothing and nobody will stop me achieving this goal. The fact that I am proactive, understand myself, can sell myself and have high standards has certainly given me the foundation to be a strong person and take a no-nonsense approach to life. I don't spend time thinking about what could be. Instead I focus on how it will be. I believe there are some key factors that make me different from other people:

I'm not Scared of Failure

Some people are scared of failure, and I can confidently say that I am not. I know that life does not always run smoothly – my father's death made me realise that. The fact that I could overcome such personal pain has taught me that I can overcome anything. I am very realistic with myself – I know I can't win everything and always have my own way – but I do know that when I experience failure it drives me to do better and prove to myself that I can do it.

When I didn't win *The Apprentice* I was a little disappointed but I knew I couldn't wallow in self-pity. I had to make the most of coming second and taking up all the opportunities my new-found fame gave me. In fact, coming second has been the best thing that's happened because it's allowed me to achieve part of my vision, which is to work for myself. Failure is part of life and everyone faces it at some time. The successful ones are those who recognise it, acknowledge it, learn from it and then move on.

I Don't Try to be Perfect

Some people want to be perfect, and anything less than that is not good enough. The fact is, however, that perfection doesn't exist. I used to stare at models in magazines wishing I could be that tall with flawless skin, long straight hair and perfect teeth. Looking at the models made me feel inadequate until I discovered that they were nothing but clotheshorses whose images were airbrushed to make everything about them seem perfect. Having seen some of the models in real life and giving interviews on television, it became apparent to me that, though some are very bright people, being a clotheshorse didn't really require too many brain cells.

The fact is that the only thing I can change about myself is my inner self. I have to live with the fact that I am five foot one with curly hair and not such perfect skin. I make the best of what I have and use my strengths to create opportunities. Nobody is perfect and trying to be so will lead to demotivation and an unfulfilled life. If you base your life on superficiality, you will get superficial results.

I'm not Narrow-minded

I like to try new things and meet people from all backgrounds regardless of their sex, race or sexual orientation. I truly believe that my open-mindedness and lack of prejudice have allowed me to live an interesting and fulfilling life. The more limits you put on yourself, the more limits you put on your life experience.

I have met a lot of people with deep-rooted prejudices: 'I don't like Jews', 'I don't like Muslims', 'I don't like women in business', 'I don't like homosexuals'. I find this very sad because it says so much more about their own values and outlook on life. Don't get me wrong. I believe everyone is entitled to their opinions, but my experience has shown me that the people who get on in life and become successful are the ones who are open-minded and happy to live without too many self-imposed barriers.

I Follow My Vision and Stay True to My Values

I was brought up with strong values. These have helped me stay true to myself and have given me an identity of which I am proud. My vision has carved out a certain path for me in life to achieve some of my dreams. I haven't always been true to myself. There have been times when I've compromised my values, which has caused me pain and, worse still, has hurt others.

Sometimes my short-sightedness has made me lose track of my vision and I have felt confused, dissatisfied and unhappy. As I've grown and matured, I have found it easier to relate to my values and use them to help me make the right decisions. My values and vision give me the focus I need, and that in turn provides me with the confidence that I am heading in the right direction. A big part of improving your condition is to set your expectations high and stretch yourself because by thinking big, you will achieve big things.

I'm Always Asking Questions

I'm always challenging my environment. I never accept things at face value. If I don't understand something, I seek out the answers; I don't wait for the answers to find me. Challenging and asking questions have helped me be more informed about people, and this has made me a better judge of character. My deeper understanding allows me to make sound decisions and to weigh up options easily and quickly. I have found that people who do not challenge get taken for a ride and miss out on opportunities.

I Have Energy and Stamina

I was in *The Apprentice* house for three months without any contact with my family and friends. I had to endure some very hard conditions, both mental and physical. Whilst some people lost the plot and their focus, my sheer energy and stamina got me through some of the hardest moments. There were times when I wanted to call it a day, but I managed to find the means to carry on. I gave every task my all. I was instrumental in all the tasks and I never took a back seat. Some of the contestants attempted to play a safe game, trying to get to the final without being seen or heard and putting in the minimum effort, but they failed. I didn't put my feet up after a long day's work either. I looked after my mind and body by running on the treadmill and letting out all the stress of the day. Tim and I were the only candidates on the show who exercised regularly; it's no coincidence that we were both in the final.

I Take Risks

I have taken a lot of risks in my life. As a child I rebelled against the restrictive ways of my culture. I always spoke out against anyone who I felt was putting me down because I was a girl and I didn't care who it was. I participated fully in British life, from joining the local sports teams to being Mary in the school Nativity play, despite the wishes of some of the conservative Muslim members of the community. This got me into trouble with my dad and other family elders, but at the same time it got me the reputation that I wasn't an easy pushover and that I would stick up for myself. In doing this I took a risk. I could have lost my family, my community and my respect, but I didn't because I was confident in what I was doing, even though others around me couldn't see my reasons.

I take risks more than other people because I always ask myself, 'If I do this what's the worst that can happen?' If the worst outcome of my risk does not harm other people or compromise my values then I will take it. The risks I have taken have served me well, such as finding a different job when I have felt demotivated or not respected; going travelling at the height of my career; giving up a full-time job to do *The Apprentice* without getting paid; marrying a man from outside my culture; and behaving in a manner that was not expected or accepted by narrow-minded people. In my opinion those who do not take a few risks in their life can miss out on achieving their goals and opening up some incredible experiences and opportunities.

I P.U.S.H. Myself

I always push for what I want and where I want to be. Being Proactive, Understanding myself and others,

Selling my strengths and having High standards are what I believe give me the strong foundation to go out in the world with confidence. Being pushy is not a crime; it's nothing to be ashamed of and has certainly never done me any harm. To P.U.S.H. yourself is to give yourself the skills to create and take advantage of opportunities. If you P.U.S.H. yourself, you will gain the confidence, self-esteem and motivation to make you a better and more successful person.

ACTION PLAN

Task 1: Record Your Successes

Start to record all the things you've done in your life that you feel have made you successful.

Update your list regularly and, over time, you will see whether you are moving forward or standing still and watching life pass you by.

Task 2: Stay Focused

Ask yourself everyday, 'What have I done today that has helped me move forward in my life?' This will keep you focused.

Task 3: Define Success

Write down what success means to you.

SUMMARY

- Identify what success means to you and recognise it when you achieve it.
- Monitor how you are doing on a yearly basis – make a list of how you are moving forward in life year on year.
- Behave and act in a manner which will get others talking about you in positive and complimentary terms.
- Don't be afraid to be successful and to be proud of it.

CONCLUSION
Don't Let Them Call You Crazy

Have you ever been in a situation where you've thought to yourself, 'Am I the only sane person in this group? Why can't they see what I can see? Is it me or is it them?' It's hard to put into words the way I've felt in situations like this. The only thing that's come close to it is the film *One Flew Over the Cuckoo's Nest*. Jack Nicholson plays an angry, misunderstood young man who gets sent to a mental institution so they can monitor whether he is in fact mad or just angry. Inside he meets patients who are all crazy to the outside world and are treated as such in the institution, but they all have their individual personality. Nicholson's character challenges the way these patients are taught and treated. It's such a powerful film. I relate to it because there have been instances in my life, both at home and at work, when people have felt I'm a little crazy because I am pushy, outspoken, energetic, competitive, enthusiastic, driven and strong. Crazy, because that's not what's expected of an Asian woman. Crazy, because it's not what the majority of people are like. And crazy, because they think they know me better than I know myself, and how dare I think above my station and have such big visions.

The fact is that no one knows you better than you know yourself. You are in control of your actions and behaviours, and you are in control of your life and what happens to you in that life. You have to take responsibility for you. If you want to learn, you can; if you're not learning, only you are stopping yourself. If you're making excuses as to why you're not learning, they are coming out of your mouth; they are convincing only yourself, no one else. You can do anything you want; you just have to find within yourself the will to do it and the vision for which to strive.

WORK HARD

Success is not handed to people on a plate and it's not easy to achieve. Understand this and realise it. I've had to work extremely hard – consistently over and above what was expected of me – to get what I want. I was not blessed with rich parents but with parents who had strong values and showed me the meaning of hard work. I know that I can always look after myself, no matter what happens. I've watched privileged people squander their parents' money and not push themselves because they knew that if the worst comes to the worst, mummy and daddy's trust fund will see them right. But what's come to my attention over and over again is that it's not money that makes people who they are; it's their standards, their vision, their values, their self-awareness and the way they relate to others. Money can never buy you self-respect; only you can achieve that by putting effort into being who and what you are.

Life is not easy, and life without a purpose is even harder. The P.U.S.H. concept has helped me give myself and my life a structure to which I can refer and make sure I'm on the right track. I do things differently to other people because I understand that my life experience is unique to me.

LIFE EXPERIENCE

There is nothing more powerful than your life experience. It's what makes you the person you are; it's how you see the world; and it's also what I believe gives people their common sense. That's why our parents and grandparents are always so useful. They may not know or understand the world we live in today and why we do the things we do, but they can always give us their experience and what they learnt from it. I don't think we respect that enough nowadays, and it's to our own detriment.

The more life experiences you have, the more you can talk about subjects with authority, and the more respect you will get from people. Some of the most intelligent people I've met have the least common sense because they've relied on their intelligence and very little else to get on in life. Let me tell you, having an intelligent brain won't get you that far if you lack social skills and common sense. What you have to do is make your life experience relevant and useful to other people, and present it in a way that others can relate to, understand and appreciate.

P.U.S.H. YOUR CHILDREN

Being Proactive, Understanding yourself, Selling yourself and having High standards will give you the confidence, insight, knowledge and motivation you need to achieve what you want. It will also positively affect the lives of people around you. Teaching children the concept of P.U.S.H. will give them a head start and prepare them for the competitive world ahead. If they have the life skills that P.U.S.H. teaches them from an early age, I believe they will be more successful than those who don't. Encourage your children to be the best they can, and help them to reflect on their success, whatever that might be – getting the grades they want, scoring the winning goal, buying what they were saving up for. Kids should be encouraged to put in the effort and to be:

- ■ Competitive
- ■ Confident
- ■ Self-aware

I meet so many parents who put their children down and say, 'Oh she's too confident,' 'He's too loud,' 'He's got too much energy,' or 'She's always asking questions,' as if these are bad traits. They are not bad traits. They are the traits of successful people, and children should be encouraged to link that behaviour with success.

IT'S ALL RIGHT TO BE PUSHY

Let me tell you one thing: if I wasn't pushy I wouldn't have written this book. People say to me, 'Do you always get what you want?' and I reply, 'Yes, if I really push for it and really want it.' Some people just don't know how to react to that. I'm not going to make any apologies for my confidence and self-belief. Why should I? I deserve everything I get because I've worked hard for it. I don't see why being pushy is bad. If I don't push and someone else does then they have a better chance of getting what I want. Why would I let someone else get what I want? Some people may say, 'Well, that's life.' My response and attitude to that is, 'No, that's your life. In my life, I make sure I put everything into getting what I want. I don't give up on myself. If I don't get it this time, I'll get it next time, but whatever happens, I will get it.'

My attitude and approach might scare some people, but that's their problem, not mine. I'm not out to scare; I'm out to get things done that will make me happy. If you're scared of that you need to analyse why. I know I can't please other people all the time so my focus is to please myself first. You have to be a little selfish to get what you want; as long as you're driven by the right values, you won't go far wrong.

TAKE TIME TO REFLECT

It's really important to take time to reflect on your life and give yourself a pat on the back for your achievements. Self-congratulation is a sign that you are in tune with who you are and are not afraid to give yourself credit where it's due. I have forgotten to do that sometimes. I've been too hard on myself, pushed myself too far and failed to recognise my achievement. It's taken me years to appreciate where I've come from and what I've achieved. Once I start to think about it I manage to say 'Well done' to myself. You have to recognise when you've achieved something important. Celebrate it and share your happiness with others. Putting your mind to something and following it through is not an easy task; it takes a certain kind of person to do that.

NOW, GET ON WITH IT

So now you have the knowledge and the insight, what are you waiting for? Get on with being a success!